HATTERAS SUMMERS

Hatteras Summers

A CHILDHOOD ON THE OUTER BANKS

Buddy Swain

— BLAIR —

To Grandmom, Pop Pop, Sister, and Mama
and all those souls past and present
who are a part of these precious memories,
and
Gee Gee Rosell, in memoriam

CONTENTS

CHAPTER 1

Going to Grandmom's by Crossing Pamlico Sound

It began as a beautiful summer day. I was eight years old. An hour after we cast off from the dock in Englehard to cross the largest body of inland water on the East Coast, Pamlico Sound, the tranquil blue sky morphed into a menacing rage of dark clouds, frequent lightning streaks, and intimidating thunderclaps. The freighter changed from smooth sailing to pitching and rolling as the weather worsened. Under the weight of the storm, the sound thrashed and growled like a restless beast, its foamy mane rose and crashed with wild rage.

Pamlico Sound separates the Outer Banks from the mainland of North Carolina. It extends some 80 miles long, stretching from Roanoke Island in the north—the site of the first permanent English colony in America—to Cedar Island in the south, where some of my early ancestors landed on this continent in the mid-1700s. It's 10 to 30 miles wide and 8 to 26 feet deep, making it a relatively shallow body of water.

My brother and I lived on the mainland with our parents in the sleepy, small town of Washington, in eastern North Carolina—not the most exciting place for two brothers who needed constant entertainment.

On that early June morning in 1951, my parents, my five-year-old brother Clifford, and I left Washington for Hatteras in my father's one-seater truck, which barely accommodated the four of us. I sat between my parents while my mother held my brother. There were no seat belts in those days. Behind the cab was a stack of mattresses on a rack suspended from one side of the truck's rails to the other—six mattresses with six matching box springs. We

Postcard of the *Hadeco* leaving the harbor and heading toward the Pamlico Sound

stored our suitcases below the mattresses in the truck's cargo bed. My father was a traveling salesman who sold beds door-to-door in rural eastern North Carolina. For him, this was a business trip and an obligatory visit with his in-laws. We drove on Highway 264 to Engelhard, where the freighter Hadeco waited at the dock.

Highway 264 between Washington and Englehard was a quiet, rural stretch of road winding through the heart of eastern North Carolina. Vast tobacco, corn, and cotton fields interspersed with patches of pine forests and swampy lowlands bordered the road. Small, unassuming towns and cross-roads dotted the route, each with a few general stores with gas pumps out front and homes scattered along the way. Farmhouses, barns, and the occasional tractor added to the pastoral charm.

During our relaxed, scenic journey, time seemed to pass slowly. To me, a road trip anywhere was thrilling. The ride to Engelhard, followed by a three-and-a-half-hour boat trip on the *Hadeco*, made the excitement even more extraordinary.

Grandmom and Pop Pop waited for us on the dock in Engelhard. The crew loaded the *Hadeco* with freight for its return trip to Hatteras. Time has erased from my memory why Grandmom was there, as she certainly didn't cross the sound that morning to meet us. Terrified of the water, she only left home once a year to visit us or see the doctor. I could read the concern on her wrinkled brow as she greeted us.

"The wind has been picking up since early morning," she said.

Milton, the captain of the *Hadeco*, reassured her that the crossing would not be too rough. She could have stayed and spent the weekend at Miss Watson's boarding house to avoid the bad weather. However, it was Friday, and the *Hadeco* would not return until the following Tuesday. Who was to say that Tuesday's weather would be any better? Milton warned us our boat ride would be rough, but none of us knew what was in store.

Milton was a native of Hatteras, a quaint village on the southern end of Hatteras Island. During the 1940s and early 1950s, he served as the captain of the *Hadeco*, crossing Pamlico Sound twice weekly with freight and passengers. This boat transported seafood, Hatteras Village's only export, to the mainland and returned with supplies for the four or five modest local mercantile businesses there.

Getting Daddy's truck on the boat was quite a feat. The freighter crewmen constructed a temporary ramp from the road to the dock using two two-by-twelve wooden planks supported underneath by stacked wooden blocks. Two additional planks spanned from the dock to the boat. The challenge was to navigate this course without driving off the makeshift ramp. One miscalculation would cause the truck to plunge into the water between the dock and the freighter. Daddy steered his truck onto the freighter's narrow deck with the precision of a brain surgeon, leaving no room to spare between the port and starboard rails. Even though the *Hadeco* was not designed to ferry vehicles, two could fit in front of its pilothouse. Daddy masterfully drove his truck on board where it fit perfectly. Pop Pop and Milton, the boat's mate, secured it to the deck to keep it from being tossed overboard during the sound crossing.

The wind picked up as we left the harbor, turning the sea a turbulent gray. After an hour, the weather worsened, and everyone sought shelter in the pilothouse. The boat pitched and rolled as each wave stressed the timbers of the wooden hull. Some passengers expressed concern for our safety, but I felt secure with my grandfather firmly holding my hand. Pop Pop (as we grandkids called him) was a waterman who had spent his life working on the water harvesting seafood, so he was used to rough seas. There was no indication from him that our safety was at risk.

After a while, the vessel pitched and rolled so violently that maintaining a steady stance was difficult. Mother decided the safest place for her and my brother was on a bottom bunk in the pilothouse. Later, my brother told me his only memory of the trip was that our mother lay so close to him that she pinned him against the inside wall of the bunk. With no room to move, he could barely breathe. The air in the pilothouse was thick with stale cigarette smoke and diesel fumes. As the choppy sound tossed the boat about, my mother cried out in fear, matching the rhythm of each oncoming wave.

No sooner had we left the dock than Grandmom became seasick. It looked like the nausea started at my Grandmom's toes and rose to her neck, accompanied by a retching sound I will never forget. She became good friends with the slop bucket Milton kept in the freighter's pilothouse. Since there was no restroom on the boat, unless you could make it to the rails to hurl into the turbulent sound, the bucket was the only option. The chaotic rhythm of the sound was not so different from the deep, strained moans of *Hadeco*'s hull bending under relentless waves. With each heave, it felt as if everything in her stomach ended up in a white porcelain slop bucket.

I dearly loved my grandmother and seeing her so sick troubled me. Pop Pop said, "For God's sake, Mag, if you keep that up, there will be nothing left of you by the time we fetch up to Hatt'ras."

Oddly, through all this, my younger brother showed no anxiety despite my mother's terrified cries, which echoed every fifteen seconds. An empty light socket hanging above him on a short wire fastened to the upper bunk drew his attention. I watched him try to poke his chubby right index finger into the socket for amusement. Mother was so consumed by fear that she overlooked his playful act. Each time he aimed at his target, the freighter would roll, throwing his arm off course and causing his finger to miss the empty socket. Each roll of the boat prevented him from being electrocuted.

About an hour into the trip, our attention shifted to my father's truck. The waves crashing over the boat's bow were soaking it. Each wave towered, curved, and broke with a tremendous roar as it slammed into the boat's bow. Wild cascades of water rushed and spilled over the bow, drenching the deck with its relentless force.

Milton shouted over the noise and commotion that the *Hadeco* was taking on too much water. "If this wind lasts much longer," he said, "we'll have to let the truck go over the side so the boat will ride higher in the water." No sooner had he spoken the words than we saw smoke billowing from the truck's cab.

Grandmom (Maggie Stowe Wade) and Pop Pop (Clifford Wolletine Wade)
sometime in the 1960s

Through the rain and wind-driven spray, Pop Pop and the mate scrambled
over cargo on the deck to reach the truck and extinguish the fire. Sparks flew,
and occasional flames flickered from under the dash of the old '38 Ford. The
boat's movement had caused hanging wires under the dash to chafe, creating
a short circuit in the electrical system. After locating the problematic wires,
the mate disconnected them from the battery, and the sparks stopped flying.
By this time, the inside of the truck was soaking wet. Needless to say, the
mattresses were getting wet as well.

Another bout of Grandma's vomiting drew everyone's attention away from
the excitement of the fire. Grandma's false teeth—both uppers and lowers—
flew out of her mouth, clattered into the bucket, and sloshed inside. As the
boat rocked, the bucket slid and skidded across the floor, crashing into the
pilothouse walls and back.

Finally, mercifully, the sound began to calm down. Daddy didn't have to push his truck and mattresses overboard. The *Hadeco* grew more stable. Mother's screams became less frequent. Grandmom stopped vomiting. My brother finally inserted his finger into the empty electrical socket, which, fortunately, was not receiving current, so he was saved from electrocution.

When we docked at Hatteras, Grandmom fished her false teeth out of the bucket, rinsed them off, put them back in her mouth, and vowed never to cross the sound again. A tow truck removed my father's disabled truck from the boat's deck. A mechanic repaired it within a week. The wet mattresses were spread out on my grandparents' lawn to dry. Afterward, Daddy loaded them back onto the truck and sold them to residents who never knew the Pamlico Sound had baptized them.

Once my brother and I made it to our grandparents' home, one adventure followed another. The beach and the emerald-green waters of the Atlantic Ocean were always there, for swimming, fishing, strolling along the surf, and collecting shells. On the sound side, we spent many afternoons at the harbor docks, where fishermen worked, unloading their daily catch. Once the harbor's activity slowed in the late afternoon, its docks become an oasis of tranquility. An emerald-green salt marsh framed the shoreline, serving as a vital refuge and food source for marine organisms. Boats rested serenely, their hulls gently nudging the docks in a lullaby as the air carried the faint, salty perfume of the sound mingled with the earthy scent of the marsh. Seagulls glided silently overhead, and the occasional ripple from a curious fish sent concentric circles spreading outward as if the harbor itself breathed in quiet contentment. This was—as still is—a haven where time slows, the world softens, and peace settles like a soothing blanket.

CHAPTER 2

Going to Grandmom's, Driving the Beach

A trip to Grandmom's, taking the *Hadeco* from Engelhard to Hatteras Village, was always a memorable experience, even on calm crossings. However, another way to reach Hatteras was to travel the mainland to Nags Head, take the *Barcelona*, a simple but reliable wooden ferry that carried cars and passengers across the often times rough waters of Oregon Inlet, and then drive the final seventy miles to Grandmom's house on the beach.

It was a hot and humid summer day in 1953. We were driving our recently purchased, secondhand, cream-colored, four-door 1949 Dodge, the first family car we ever owned. In its time, experts described it as a classic embodiment of midcentury American automotive design, with its bold, sweeping lines and chrome accents that gleamed under the sun. The broad and solid body exuded a sense of robust reliability. At the same time, the curved fenders and grille gave it a stately presence on the road. The 1949 Dodge captured the essence of postwar optimism, blending strength with a touch of sophisticated Americana. By the time we owned it, the car was neither stately nor reliable; the previous owners had neglected and poorly maintained it.

That day, in the heat, we were twenty-some miles from Oregon Inlet and had forty miles to go before arriving at Grandmom's house. The nearest service station was in Buxton, a small village near the island's cape.

There was nothing to do but stop the car and turn off the motor, which meant inviting another challenge to an already over-challenged automobile getting stuck in the soft sand. Today, a simple call on the cell phone to AAA and roadside assistance would be coming. But this is now, and that was then.

The ferry *Barcelona* approaches the Hatteras shore to be loaded with cars
and return north across Oregon Inlet. (Courtesy of Randell Holmes Collection,
Outer Banks History Center)

Then, on that day, even if our car was operating, we faced the challenge of
traveling those forty miles without a roadway. The only route was the berm
of the beach, an area between the tide line and the dunes. The berm is a
peaceful expanse of shifting sands and delicate textures, its golden hues
transforming with the sun's changing gaze. To me, the berm was not only
our path to Grandmom's, it was the home of the ghost crab. Ghost crabs are
pale, sand-colored creatures perfectly camouflaged against the shore.

Thanks to its long, spindly legs supporting its compact, boxy body, a ghost
crab can dart sideways with fantastic speed. Its stalked eyes often turn to look
around, and it moves with careful curiosity, one claw slightly bigger than the
other. Usually seen scurrying between the tideline and its burrow, the ghost
crab is a fleeting and elusive presence, a tiny sentinel of the beach's quiet,
windswept ecosystem. And nearby, swaying in the breeze, are little tufts of

sea oats and grasses occasionally near the dunes. This zone feels alive with tranquil energy, a peaceful buffer between the ocean's influence and the stability of the land.

We timed the trip so it would be low tide when we landed on the south side of Oregon Inlet. That gave us, for the most part, a broad, firm beach to drive on for the forty miles south to Buxton. A welcome asphalt road greeted us for the remaining twenty miles of our journey to Hatteras Village. There was an alternative to the open beach "highway." On the island's sound side was an unpaved, single-lane track with very loose sand, deep ruts, and patches of mud and water holes—not much of an option. So, the best way to avoid getting stuck was to reduce our tires' air pressure to 18 pounds per square inch and opt for the beach.

Once my father accelerated the car to 20 mph, he was reluctant to slow down or stop until we reached Buxton. Moving at this speed, the old Dodge would plane across areas of soft sand much like a fast-moving boat does over water. Slowing down or stopping invited the possibility of getting stuck, which was still very likely since the car didn't have four-wheel drive.

Everyone knew to relieve themselves behind the nearest dune before beginning this risky trek since official rest areas did not exist. My little brother Clifford, who, even at five years of age, liked to do things dramatically, always chose to relieve himself from the top of the highest dune he could find. He enjoyed improving his marksmanship and distance from lofty peaks. He thought that if he peed straight ahead from the top of the dune, he would pee further than simply straight forward at the base of one. Once he finished, he could not turn down one last chance to expend some energy before being imprisoned for the next two hours in the car's back seat. Taking advantage of his position on the dune's crest, he faked a fall, followed by a joyful tumble to the bottom of the dune, laughing and screaming. When gravity could not carry him farther, he lay at the bottom of the dune, a ball of human flesh with sand stuck in every crack and crevice of his still giggling body. Our parents undoubtedly disapproved of his antics. Regret soon set in when the discomfort of sand clinging to Clifford's already hot, sweaty body overshadowed the thrill of rolling down the dune, and there was no chance of escaping his misery until we arrived at Grandmom's house.

That day, the first fifteen miles were uneventful. The beach was wide and flat, and the sand was firm. Miles of undisturbed golden beach lay in front of us, with the blue Atlantic rushing by on our left and windswept dunes topped with golden sea oats whizzing by on our right. While cruising along the flat beach, we sometimes encountered a series of sand formations created by wind and surf action that I called "camelbacks." We thought riding over them was like being on a roller coaster. My brother and I submitted to the forces of physics as we were tossed around in the back seat. We frequently grabbed the back of the front seat to avoid bumping our heads on the car's roof. Clifford and I had never experienced a carnival ride that brought more gales of laughter and ear-to-ear smiles.

The car provided shelter from the hot summer sun, and the breeze through its windows kept us comfortable—except for my sandy little brother.

If the trip went smoothly, the iconic Cape Hatteras Lighthouse would come into view after about an hour and a half of steady travel. This iconic lighthouse is a beacon known for its distinctive black-and-white spiral design. It is the tallest lighthouse in the United States, rising 198 feet. The Corps of Engineers constructed it around 1868 to warn sailors of the treacherous Diamond Shoals, a twelve-mile-long sandbar off the coast that has caused numerous shipwrecks, earning the area the nickname "Graveyard of the Atlantic." Being the first person to spot the lighthouse always gave this ten-year-old a profound sense of accomplishment, so I maintained a constant vigil from the beginning of the journey, even though this famous landmark was forty miles away. However, we weren't there yet . . .

About twenty minutes into the trip, my father noticed the temperature gauge on the car's dashboard was registering hot. A few miles later, he stopped the steaming car on a substantial section of the beach. "Son of a bitch," rolled from my father's lips. I heard him say God so often that I was unsure whether he was praying or cussing—but cussing would be my guess! Steam poured from under the hood. My dad knew this was an unmistakable signal of trouble, a cry for attention from the engine's heart. There was not another soul in sight. The hot July summer sun blazed overhead like a relentless fire. The air shimmered with heat, rising in wavy distortions from the sand, while every surface it touched felt scalding to the touch. The car urgently needed to be repaired because the flowing tide would be lapping around its wheels in a few hours. A high tide would undermine our vehicle, so the ocean's waves might wash it into the sea.

Mama took us kids walking on the beach while my father examined the problem with the cooling system. The midday heat was practically unbearable.

Everyone was concerned except my little brother. He seized this opportunity to eliminate the aggravating sand clinging to his skin. He ran the few steps to the Atlantic Ocean, where he could wash away the grit. My brother understood he shouldn't jump into the surf, but he did it anyway. He also knew he shouldn't have rolled down that dune where he had aimed at and tinkled on an unfortunate ghost crab. I'm sure the ghost crab was never the same, and neither was my little brother's bottom after our father spanked him for taking a midday plunge without permission. That day, he seemed to trade one discomfort for another. He cried from the pain of his thrashing, my mother cried from her fear of the uncertainty of our predicament, and I teared up because everyone else did—except for my father.

He had discovered our trouble. It stemmed not from a hole in the radiator but a small hose leak at one end near a fitting. He used his pocketknife to cut away the defective part of the hose. Fortunately, there was enough remaining hose to stretch it to where he needed to reattach it. I thought nothing else stood in the way of continuing our trip. However, there was one crucial detail: we needed water to refill a bone-dry radiator.

Saltwater was available everywhere, but not a drop of fresh water anywhere. Water from the ocean would mean disaster for a motor, but not immediately. Salt in the water is highly corrosive to metal, accelerating the rusting and degradation of the cooling system's radiator, engine block, and other metal components. The chance of someone coming to help us was slim; someone showing up along with fresh water increased the odds. Realizing this, my father did what anyone else in the same predicament would do. He found a jug in the flotsam on the beach and filled it with seawater. After several trips to the ocean's edge, Daddy topped off the radiator with ocean water. Seawater would get us to Grandmom's house. Still, it would also mean the inevitable demise of our only means of transportation.

Sometime after my father bought the Dodge, I heard him mumbling to himself and telling my mother what a lemon he thought it was. He was constantly fixing something. If it wasn't the universal joint, it was the starter or the generator. I heard him exclaim repeatedly, "It's been nothing but trouble! I wish the son-of-a-bitch who sold it to me had it crammed up his damn ass." My father never strayed from using direct and vivid language to express his feelings when upset.

My father constantly bragged about the Dodge to his friends, especially to the man who had sold it to him, because he never wanted to appear as if someone had scammed him. However, he was sure the salesman deliberately sold him an automobile of questionable performance.

The following week, when we returned home from Hatteras with a car whose cooling system still contained coolant from the Atlantic Ocean, he bragged about how great the vehicle had performed on the trip. He never told anyone about the incident on the beach.

In fact, in less than a week, he returned to the used car lot and found the salesman who sold him the car. Daddy said that although it "ran like a top," he needed a car with only two doors because he feared his sons might mistakenly open one of the doors while riding in the back seat. He didn't want us to fall out and get hurt. It must have seemed like a valid reason to the salesman because my father's bragging convinced him the car was not a lemon. He traded even for a Buick, a two-door hardtop, a much sportier car than the Dodge, and one whose cooling system had never tasted so much as a drop of saline water from the mighty Atlantic.

CHAPTER 3

Going to the Store

"Now, son, you go straight to the store and hurry back as quickly as possible. I can't start dinner until you get back." Those were the last words from Grandmom as I left her at the end of the path on my way to the store. She emphasized "hurry" and "quick." Grandmom never bought perishable groceries for more than one meal at a time. She didn't have a refrigerator for the first half of her life. Even after my grandfather bought their first one, the old habit of not shopping ahead of time was hard to break.

For everyone except Pop Pop, breakfast at her house usually consisted of buttered toast and coffee. His morning meal also included bacon, eggs, and cheese. He arose every morning at 2:30 a.m., except on Sundays, to fish his nets. Grandmom prepared the same breakfast menu for him for sixty-five of their seventy years of marriage.

Pop Pop began fishing at the age of twelve. It was the only life he knew—grueling work and low pay. He was physically robust and muscular, with a build shaped by the rugged, repetitive labor involved in his trade. His shoulders and arms were powerful, a well-defined testament to the physical labor of driving stakes by hand, setting nets, and hauling fish into a boat. After fishing with his nets, sorting the fish, and selling them at one of the various fish houses along the harbor, he would return home for dinner, which Grandmom always served at 11:00 a.m. sharp unless she encountered circumstances beyond her control. Dinner is what we call our midday meal.

When it was time for Grandmom to prepare dinner, I knew I might as well stop whatever I was doing. She always called me in from playing and sat me

Mr. Dolph's store and the Weather Bureau (right).
(Photo courtesy of the Burrus Family)

beside her at the kitchen table. There, she made a grocery list of the items
she needed. Her handwriting was a work of art. I watched her write the list
with envy. She held the pencil steadily, and her writing was beautiful. After
finishing, she removed only the portion of paper on which she had written
from the tablet. She stored the rest of the sheet with its tablet in the upper
drawer of her sideboard, where it would be used again later in the afternoon
before supper. "Waste not, want not" was her motto. Supper is what we call
our third meal of the day.

My task was to carry the list to the store and return home as quickly as
possible with the food supplies. This seven-year-old boy was easily distracted from his chores, so picking up groceries presented an opportunity
for adventure.

The store was less than a fifth of a mile from our house. Walking there,
handing the list to a clerk who gathered the items, charging them to Pop
Pop's account, and returning home should have taken only fifteen minutes.
On rare occasions, it would take me an hour. Today was one of those days.

When I left for the store, it was high tide. Mud fiddlers moved from the
salt marsh, covering the path from the front yard to the sandy road. The male
fiddlers' giant claws looked as big as hedge clippers. The only way I would
walk down the path, teeming with what I imagined were aggressive, blood-

thirsty crabs, was if someone held my hand and walked with me. Grandmom walked me safely to the road. I was sure that by the time I returned from the store, the tide would have fallen enough for the fiddlers to go back to the marsh, where they would be out of sight. And for me, out of sight was out of mind. It was several years later before I finally outgrew this fear.

Mud fiddlers aside, I had a job to do. Walking along a deep, sandy road felt like an endless uphill struggle. With each step, my feet sank into the loose sand, forcing me to exert more effort to lift my legs and move forward. The sand shifted unpredictably underfoot, making it difficult to find stable footing and causing my balance to waver with every step. Walking in the packed sand of the tire ruts on the unpaved road was much easier. The trek became tiresome whenever a slow-moving car forced me out of these ruts and onto the loose, powder-fine sand, where I sank to my ankles and slowed to a snail's pace. There were areas where the sun's intense rays heat the sand to an almost unbearable temperature. The hot sand burned my feet, making me hop from one patch of vegetation to another alongside the road to soothe my sensitive feet. There was a low spot in the road just before I reached Miss Ursa's house, where rain from the night before had left an inviting puddle of water. I couldn't resist. I didn't realize that splashing around and wading would extend the trip I was supposed to finish quickly.

Mr. Nelson and Miss Ursa were my grandparents' neighbors. Their house was a picturesque scene of tranquility: a whitewashed, one-and-a-half-story home built at the turn of the twentieth century, with a large manicured front lawn nestled among a thicket of live oaks, their branches draped with Spanish moss. As I approached their home, Mr. Nelson and some friends were playing croquet on the front lawn. I lingered at the edge of the road in the gentle summer breeze beside a storm-gnarled red cedar. For ten minutes or more, I witnessed an exciting and competitive sporting event. The charming natural setting made me pause to appreciate its beauty.

Next came the village barbershop. The barber, Mr. Damon, was not cutting hair but sitting on his shop's front porch. He was whittling a piece of wood into the image of a shorebird. His talent mesmerized me. It seemed like no time passed before the piece of wood was shaped into a goose. Mr. Damon eventually asked me where I was heading. I told him I was on one of Grandmom's grocery missions. He encouraged me to keep walking.

Just past the barbershop stood the famous Hatteras Weather Bureau. Cape Hatteras, where the Gulf Stream and Labrador Current converge, is

Mr. Dolph on the porch of his store, circa 1940. (Photo
courtesy of the Burrus Family)

crucial for weather forecasting. The current building was commissioned and
opened on January 1, 1902. I always paused to gaze at the weather flags that
alerted islanders to impending conditions. A solid red pendant indicated a
small craft warning. Two pendants signified a gale warning. A square red flag
with a black square center warned of a tropical storm. Two square flags indicated a hurricane warning. That day, I watched the weatherman gather data
from instruments housed in a white louvered box on the front lawn. Afterward, he launched a weather balloon equipped with a device that transmits

pressure, temperature, and relative humidity data. What a spectacle! It took at least ten minutes before the balloon vanished, allowing me to continue on finally to the store.

Mr. Dolph's general store featured a spacious front porch that extended across the entire front of the building. My great-grandfather and his cousin, Mr. Dolph's father-in-law, founded the store in 1866, shortly after the Civil War. It has undergone several changes since then eventually evolving into a modern convenience store, The Village Market, but at this time, it stood as a two-story structure covered in white asbestos tiles. The store was located on the first floor, while the second floor served as the home for Mr. Dolph's son, Bill, and his family. There was hardly ever a moment when someone wasn't sitting on a bench on the porch, chatting with customers as they went about their daily tasks. People often sat in its shade to escape the summer sun's heat.

I spotted Mr. Victor sitting on the porch, who, for me, spelled trouble. He always seemed to be around whenever I went to the store alone. Like my grandfather, Mr. Victor loved chewing tobacco. Pop Pop started chewing at three years old, and I'm sure Mr. Victor was no different. Seeing the satisfaction he got from shifting the plug of tobacco from one cheek to the other before spitting out the juice made me want to try it.

Occasionally, I would sneak a small leaf from Pop Pop's tobacco plug, which he kept on the table behind his rocking chair in the sitting room of his home. His favorite brand was Apple tobacco. I often hid in the upper branch of an oak tree in the front yard with my stash. When I was sure no one was watching, I slipped it into my mouth and chewed. I tried to savor the burning, piercing flavor. All I got from the experience was a gag reflex so intense that I immediately spat it out. I figured I must be chewing it wrong. Fortunately, I never discovered what it actually was.

At any rate, Mr. Victor's favorite pastime was to spit tobacco juice on children's bare toes as they passed by the corner of the porch where he sat. He always seemed to hit his target, no matter where he had to aim. From experience, I knew that if I tried to avoid his spittle attack, he would calmly remove the moist plug from his cheek and throw it at me. It was better to pass close to him and risk his tobacco juice missing my feet than to risk a plug aimed straight at my head. As I approached, I jumped and danced around as if I were walking on hot coals, trying to evade his deadly aim, but he hit his mark anyway. The feeling of slimy tobacco spittle between my toes made my skin crawl. His sense of accomplishment was directly proportional to my displeasure. The bigger the fuss I made, the harder he laughed.

Despite everything, I always liked Mr. Victor. If he wasn't teasing me with his tobacco quirks, he was a charming, toothless older man whose long nose nearly touched his protruding chin when his mouth was closed. His tanned face, skin almost leather from years of sun exposure, and his belly laugh, which erupted from deep within when he made me do my avoidance dance, reminded me of a character from one of my childhood storybooks. Even today, when I visit the site of Mr. Dolph's general store, I miss Mr. Victor's distinctive way of showing affection.

Once I finally made it into the store, I handed my grocery list to my aunt, who worked there as a clerk. My mother always called her Sister, and I did the same. Sister was Pop Pop's unmarried daughter. She lived with my grandparents and really was a surrogate caregiver for my brother and me during our summers at Hatteras. She was the kindest, gentlest, sweetest person I had ever known—and also the slowest. Sister didn't rush for anyone. She worked steadily, completed her tasks, and did them correctly without hurrying. Before she gathered the few items on Grandmom's list, I convinced her to buy me an ice cream bar, which she insisted I eat before returning home. We both knew Grandmom didn't want me to eat anything that might spoil my dinner.

Returning home, I encountered all the same distractions again, but in reverse. I knew I was in trouble when I heard Grandmom shouting my name across the nearby salt marsh. As I turned onto the path that led to the house, I saw Grandmom wearing her faded ankle-length frock, protected by a bibbed apron, and also wearing a concerned expression. She was pacing back and forth on the pizer, the old timer's term for the porch, wringing her hands and calling my name at the top of her lungs.

My safety wasn't a concern for Grandmom. She knew that a child anywhere in Hatteras Village during the '40s and '50s was as safe as he would be in his mother's arms. Adults throughout the village looked after each other's children, ensuring their safety and good behavior.

No, her concern was the time. My grandmother felt she had to have dinner on the table by 11:00 sharp. No one expected that of her, not even Pop Pop, who hadn't eaten since early morning. A self-imposed curse compelled her to be prompt and made her anxious if dinner wasn't ready on time.

As much as I wanted to run to the house, I couldn't. The mud fiddlers were still on the path, and there was no way I would walk through them alone. I couldn't finish this last leg of the journey with them there. I could tell by the tone of Grandmom's shouting that she was annoyed with me for holding up dinner. I worried she was upset with me for being late, and I was so terrified by the sight of all those mud fiddlers on the path that I started crying.

Grandmom stepped down from the pizer, waded through the fiddlers, and met me on the road. Even though I was the reason she served dinner an hour late, she leaned over, kissed me on the forehead, wrapped her arms around me, and escorted me safely back to the house.

At three o'clock that afternoon, Grandmom went out on the pizer and motioned for me to come inside the house. I climbed down from a limb in the old oak tree in the front yard, where I imagined I was piloting an airplane flying over the island. She was sitting at the kitchen table when I entered the room. She had prepared her grocery list and handed it to me. "Son, it's almost time for supper," she said, "and I need a few things from the store. Please take this list, rush straight to the store, and come back as fast as you can. I can't start supper until you return." There was the familiar emphasis on "rush" and "fast."

It was low tide. The path from the house to the road was clear of fiddler crabs. She planned to serve supper at 4:00 p.m. sharp unless faced with circumstances beyond her control, like things that might distract me along the way.

CHAPTER 4

Going to the Landing

I was startled by the tone of Grandmom's voice. She was in a panic and very upset. The words burst into my upstairs bedroom window from the yard below: "My blessed, how in the world am I going to get my clothes dry?" It was Monday morning, washday, and Grandmom's effort to finish that weekly chore had come to a stop. This was before the days of indoor drying appliances. Grandmom's voice shattered the peaceful silence of my bedroom: "My clothesline is gone. Whatever will I do?"

My grandmother was a creature of habit, and you could set your watch by her routines. This did not just apply to mealtimes. There was a time for everything. A time to rise each morning; a time to fix breakfast; a time to eat breakfast; a time to wash the breakfast dishes; a time to go to the cistern to ladle a bucket of water and bring it into the kitchen; a time to straighten the house; a time to make the beds; a time to comb her white, waist-length hair, braid it, and roll it into a bun at the back of her head; a time to run across the road to visit her sister, Kate; a time to return home and prepare dinner; a time to eat dinner; a time to wash the dinner dishes; a time to sit quietly and read the Bible; a time to rock on the pizer; a time to run across the road for another visit with Kate, this time on her front porch where passersby would always stop and chat before continuing their journey either up or down the road; a time to return home and prepare supper; a time to eat supper; a time to wash the supper dishes; a time to swing on the pizer and unwind from a long day of keeping to her schedule; a time to go inside out of the night air and mosquitoes; a time to entertain company from the village who would

Grandmom's clothesline

pop in to spin some yarns of times gone by or catch her up on the local gossip; and a time to go to bed. Those were her daily activities from Monday to Saturday. Sunday was a day of rest. A missing clothesline could disrupt her entire week's schedule. And everyone else had to share in Grandmom's misery when her schedule was off.

I rolled over in bed, placed my pillow over my head to block out any further announcements she might broadcast to the neighborhood, and pretended to be asleep. I had been worried all weekend about what had happened to her clothesline, but I could not yet bring myself to confess my sin to her. I decided to fake an illness, hoping to distract her from questioning me about the missing line. I had known she would say no if I'd asked for permission to use it. Without that clothesline, I'd have been an observer, not a participant, in Friday night's adventure at the landing. While being an observer was enjoyable, it lacked the thrill of participation.

Grandmom wasn't the only creature of habit on Hatteras Island; I was too. Now that I think about it, what choice did I have? It wasn't just hereditary but also environmental. Grandmom had followed her routine for over fifty years before I started spending summers with her, Pop Pop, and Sister, my aunt. Although my presence likely disrupted her daily activities, I quickly discovered that life was much sweeter when I organized my schedule to avoid interfering with her customs. Thus, her habits shaped mine.

One of my habits was to go to the landing on Friday evenings shortly after supper and stay until just before Grandmom's bedtime at nine o'clock—and not a minute later. The landing was the local name for the village harbor, which included fish houses, an ice plant, and docks. Before the early 1950s, the harbor was little more than a wide stretch of a creek that cut through part of the salt marsh on the village's western side. Its mouth emptied into Pamlico Sound.

My absence from home during Grandmom's usual after-dinner swing on the porch, followed by her visiting with company in the living room, didn't disrupt the routine. However, she could only go to bed if everyone she expected to be home was there. To avoid worrying Grandmom, whom I loved dearly, I always returned from the landing on Friday nights just before her bedtime, even if Ralph was reeling in a big catch.

The landing at Hatteras was my real-life Sea World—a realm brimming with marine life and the genuine charm of the locals. There was always some lively activity—whether it offered a new lesson about the ecosystem or captivated you with its raw, unfiltered allure. Each day was unique. The best part was that it didn't cost a dime. You didn't have to worry about staying close to an adult to protect yourself from being approached by a stranger or getting lost in a crowd. There were no shuttles, big parking lots, long lines for the next attraction, and no navigating through traffic to get to an unfamiliar bed in a strange hotel at the end of the day. Whenever boredom crept in during my summer at Grandmom's house, the landing became my go-to escape.

Several fish houses and an ice plant lined the eastern side of the creek where it opened into Pamlico Sound. Oddly enough, this plant was the village's only source of electricity for many years. Before the ice plant existed, watermen had to transport large blocks of ice from the mainland in the hulls of their freight boats. This necessity preserved the freshness of seafood, the island's primary export and source of income—several wharves extended from these functional yet straightforward fish houses along the creek bank. Here, local boat captains secured their vessels to unload the catch of the day or temporarily store supplies from the mainland, which were then distributed to local merchants. Similarly, fishermen eagerly shipped fresh seafood across the sound to markets on the mainland. It was a hub of activity every day of the week except Sunday.

Mornings brought a flurry of activities as fishermen returned from their pound nets in the sound. I spent many days sitting on the docks, waiting for the watermen's arrival, straining my eyes as I scanned the western horizon. Slowly, tiny white specks transformed into inboard-motor fishing boats laden to the washboards with spots, croakers, mullets, hogfish, trout,

Watermen unloading the catch while local boys share a few tall tales
in Hatteras harbor, 1940s

and various other commercial and noncommercial species. Pop Pop was always on one of those boats.

He fished for a living until he retired at the age of sixty-five. One day, after walking home from fishing, he fainted, and the local doctor advised him to quit. He diagnosed the issue as a heart attack, and his only treatment was this advice: "Mr. Clifford," he said, "if you continue to fish, it will kill you." That day, Pop Pop gave up fishing, a passion he cherished, following the doctor's recommendation.

The next week, he took a job at one of the fish houses, where he culled fish, weighed them, and packed them in wooden boxes lined with ice. Once filled, these boxes weighed over one hundred pounds. He arranged the heavy containers filled with fish, crabs, shrimp, and other edible sea life against the back wall of the fish house in rows, often stacking them as high as his shoulders. When there was enough seafood to load onto one of the local freight boats for transport to the mainland for sale, he single-handedly loaded the cargo onto the vessel. The work was more strenuous than fishing, but he believed he was following the doctor's orders to avoid fishing. He continued in this line of work until he was nearly eighty. On a crisp October evening, just before bedtime, he suffered his first undeniable heart attack. It took his life. He was ninety-three.

At the docks, I discovered the incredible variety of organisms that thrive in the sound—fish, crabs, shrimp, turtles, and shellfish. During that time, I learned the joy of sharing through example. When the fishermen arrived to sell their catch, anyone in the village who wanted seafood for dinner or supper needed only to show up for a free supply. I remember these common generosities as something the fishermen did without any fuss and with joy.

Afternoons at the landing were quieter than mornings. By then, fish for the market was prepared and completed. The fishermen were scattered along the shore, mending their nets for another day. Older men gathered in small groups along the docks, busy whittling juniper into a pile of shavings or spinning tales of the past. They passed down their stories and their skills to the youth loitering nearby.

The fishermen's practice was to dump tons of unsellable scrap fish overboard in the harbor. The dead organisms were a scavenger's delight.

Decaying fish floating on the creek's surface never deterred the local kids from taking an afternoon dip. On rare occasions, the boys and a few girls seized the lazy afternoon for a swim in the harbor. I wanted to join them, but Grandmom told me not to swim "in that nasty water," and I listened to her. Frequent trips to the beach to swim in the clean ocean satisfied my desire to jump into the harbor. I enjoyed sitting and watching the local teenagers as they splashed around in the fishy-smelling water. Diving from tall pilings and flipping through the air often resulted in landing on their backs or stomachs. These antics were far more entertaining to watch and certainly less painful than participating. The one time I got permission to take an afternoon plunge, I ended up with a throat infection that lasted most of the summer. I learned my lesson and never swam there again.

These dead fish also sparked thrilling entertainment. Many late afternoons, when the noise of daily activities at the docks subsided and scrap fish floated on the creek's surface for most of the day, we could see the dorsal fins of sharks breaking the water's surface in the sound beyond the harbor mouth. The scrap fish drifting in the harbor seemed to act as magnets that ultimately drew them in. What the crabs and other scavengers did not consume during the day, the sharks devoured at night. Sand sharks over six feet long sometimes stirred the water as they fed on the leftover scraps of the day. What a sight it was! I always hurried to finish supper so I could return

Quiet evening at the docks, 1940s

to the landing for the shark encounter. The next day, the harbor would be spotless, free of any trace of floating organic debris—a powerful example of how a small community and nature coexist perfectly.

Most local kids would arrive at the docks on Friday evenings around dusk. Many would take bets from others, claiming they could swim across the creek among the feeding sharks and return alive. With bets placed, several boys would strip naked, dive from the highest piling on the ice plant dock, and swim to the other side of the harbor. Dorsal fins and white butts cutting the surface of the water were a regular Friday night occurrence. To my knowledge, a shark has never harmed anyone, and a swimmer has never hurt a shark.

It was always inevitable that the evening would be exciting when Ralph arrived at the docks with his rod and reel. He was a local man of average height who became one of the first surf fishing guides when tourists first discovered Hatteras. Late in the evening, armed with a heavy-duty rod and reel featuring a strong line, a nine-foot wire leader, and a #10/0 hook, he caught stingrays and sharks as a hobby. I never saw Marlin Perkins or Stan Brock on Mutual of Omaha's *Wild Kingdom* do anything more thrilling than what I witnessed with Ralph after sunset on the piers in front of the fish houses at Hatteras Harbor.

One breezy night, after baiting his hook with two large fish and casting his line overboard, Ralph decided he wanted a cigarette while waiting for a bite. He released the brake on his reel and walked to the fish house, letting the line drop onto the dock's surface. The fish house on the dock provided the only shelter from the wind, allowing him to light up his Lucky Strike. No sooner had he placed the cigarette in his mouth when the line began to slip from his reel, producing a high-pitched whine.

Something had taken his bait. Panicked, Ralph dropped his cigarette and match, then flipped the lever to engage the reel's brake. Instantly, there was a tremendous tug on his rod, which threw him off balance, landing him on his butt in an upright sitting position. He held the rod for dear life as whatever was at the end of his line dragged him fifty feet—the length of the pier—his bottom picking up every splinter in its path. I was sure he was about to be pulled off the pier by whatever was on the other end of his line. By the time he reached the end of the pier, he had the presence of mind to release the reel's brake, stopping just short of being pulled into the shark-infested, foul-smelling creek. Like a true champion, he managed to stand, brace himself against a large piling, and reengage the brake. He fought the monster at the other end of the line for what felt like an hour.

At no point during the fight did Ralph complain about the splinters and bruises he received from his unexpected and potentially dangerous trip to the end of the pier. Ralph could guess what was on his line when the creature stopped swimming and settled at the bottom of the creek. No matter how hard Ralph pulled on the rod, it would not budge. It stubbornly remained there for fifteen minutes before resuming its struggle.

"I think I have a big stingray," Ralph said. He was right.

It was the largest stingray I had ever seen, measuring about four feet from the tip of one wing to the tip of the other. No sooner was the flapping creature lifted from the water and placed belly-side up on the dock than it started giving birth to six babies. They emerged from the stingray's cloaca at the base of her tail and slid onto the pier, marking my first time witnessing a live birth. The babies were perfectly formed miniature stingrays. I wanted to toss them overboard, but Ralph said, "No. There are plenty of them out there already." "Catch and release" wasn't practiced back then; people were less attuned to the ecological impact of their actions.

It took a long time for the stingray to die. Whenever I thought the ray had finally passed, she flapped her wings vigorously against her belly and the dock. Ralph cut off her tail, which had two barbed stingers. He carefully removed them—his trophy from the night's encounter. I couldn't wait to get home and tell Grandmom, Pop Pop, and Sister about what I had witnessed.

It's hard to describe the compulsion that arose in me that night. I had to catch a shark or stingray of my own. As I planned to satisfy this urge, I realized several obstacles were in my way. I didn't have the strength to fight an animal the size of the stingray that had sent Ralph flying to the pier's edge, nor did I believe I could land a shark as big as the ones I had seen in the harbor. I certainly didn't want to be pulled into the water. Even if I had the strength, I didn't own a rod and reel. For days, the craving to catch a shark continued to haunt me. Then, one day, a brilliant idea struck me while I walked from the outdoor toilet back to the house, passing Grandmom's clothesline. That clothesline was what I needed to catch a shark. I could borrow it and return it on Friday night when I got back. Grandmom would never miss it since she only used the clothesline on Mondays.

I took down the clothesline before supper to avoid wasting time before walking to the landing. I found a stainless-steel leader, a large swivel, and a hook measuring about 3 inches from its eye to the curve—all I needed to land my prize.

As I approached the dock that night, my heart was racing. I felt even more excited when one of my friends announced, "The sharks are already feeding in the creek." I quickly started assembling my fishing gear. With the help of an experienced buddy, I attached the hook to the leader, the leader to the swivel, and the swivel to Grandmom's clothesline. I baited the hook with two scrap fish. I had asked one of the fishermen for them that morning and had stored the bait in a cool spot beneath one of the docks to keep it fresh for that night. Knowing I could never control the clothesline with a shark or stingray attached, I tied one end to a slender piling at the end of the pier. Since the piling was only four or five inches in diameter, it would flex, relieving some of the tension in the line, much like Ralph's rod did the night he caught the stingray. This setup would also hopefully keep me from being pulled overboard when the big one struck.

I twirled the baited hook and leader above my head, much like a cowboy does with a lasso. When the bait had enough momentum, I let go, sending it, along with the trailing clothesline, toward the middle of the creek. Half of the line was uncoiled as it followed the bait. The plan was to let the animal, once it took the bait, run with it until the supply of line on the pier was exhausted. I figured the tension in the line tugging against the flexing piling would eventually wear the creature down. Once drained of energy, pulling it to the dock would be easy. With a gaff I'd borrowed from one of the fish houses, I'd hook the weary critter in the jaw or gills and lift it onto the pier with my buddy's help. I would return the clothesline, and Grandmom would never know the versatility of her Monday morning necessity. What could be simpler?

It didn't take long before the line began to move in the water. Something was tugging at my bait. My heart leaped! I could barely catch my breath—then, in an instant, the line on the dock surged, uncoiling with incredible speed, like a wild bolt of energy racing toward the horizon! The tension in the line made the piling flex forward. Then, there was a sharp crack, like a bullwhip cracking. The line snapped effortlessly right before my disbelieving eyes, vanishing into thin air, before I realized what had happened. After a few diminishing oscillations, the piling returned to its resting position—Grandmom's clothesline shot into the sound with my prized catch of the day still attached. I couldn't believe what had just occurred. How could I have known that the old #3 cotton crab line she used for a clothesline had suffered from dry rot?

I didn't have the money to replace the clothesline. In my childish state of mind, I decided to lie low, hoping the unfortunate event would fade away. I chose to stay in bed the following Monday morning and pretend to be sick. As planned, my feigned illness kept Grandmom from asking me about the missing clothesline. That morning, she solved her problem by spreading her weekly laundry on some yaupon and myrtle bushes growing near the yard's edge. She used to dry her clothes this way before having the convenience of a clothesline.

When Pop Pop returned home from fishing his nets, she sent him back down the road to the store to buy her a new clothesline.

The new line was a significant improvement over the old one. The following Friday night, I proudly hauled in a six-foot shark. This time, I returned the clothesline before Monday morning so Grandmom wouldn't find it missing when she came out to hang her Monday wash.

CHAPTER 5

Going Clamming

As a college sophomore, I sat in a zoology lecture on echinoderms—the spiny-skinned animals—when I suddenly understood something that had puzzled me for years: an incident from the first time I went clamming with my grandfather. My lifelong fascination with sea life meant the professor had my complete attention that day.

His lecture began with a list of traits common to members of the phylum Echinodermata—the "spiny-skin" animals. To illustrate his points, he proudly showed 35mm slides of starfish, serpent stars, sea urchins, and sea lilies—all photographed during his research dives. Amid the flicker and hum of the projector, each image served as a small portal to another world. Before the lecture ended, I would find in those "spiny-skin" animals the echo of a memory I'd carried for years.

Toward the end of the lecture, the professor discussed Holothuroidea—the class that includes sea cucumbers. Projected onto a large screen at the front of the lecture hall, filled with 249 sleepy students and one wide-awake, me, was a creature I had seen once before, at age ten.

It was hard for me to understand how 249 students could sleep through Dr. Lehman's description of evisceration—a defense mechanism used by sea cucumbers. I nudged the dozing student next to me, hoping at least one other person would appreciate what was being shared. My startled classmate, however, didn't share my enthusiasm. Looking back, I suppose my excitement only makes sense if you've gone clamming with Pop Pop—and been on the receiving end of one of his pranks.

Counting the morning's catch of clams

In moments of threat, sea cucumbers eviscerate—that is, they expel their internal organs, which resemble intestines, from their bodies. These smooth, fleshy organs, surprisingly large relative to the animal's size, often become a more tempting target for predators than the sea cucumber itself. While a predator—such as a blue crab—feeds on the discarded organs, the sea cucumber makes a slow escape, later regenerating its lost innards and surviving to eviscerate another day. This remarkable defense can also be triggered by a sudden impact on the animal's elongated body.

My grandfather, whom my brother and I affectionately called Pop Pop, started fishing at age twelve to help support his parents. When he wasn't out on the water, he earned extra money clamming—a pastime he loved dearly. He often clammed from 7 a.m. to 3 p.m. without stopping, hauling in as many as 1,400 clams on a good day. Even on his worst days, he rarely caught fewer than 800.

After returning to shore, he counted the clams. He packed them into burlap bags, which he slung over his shoulder and carried on foot for half a mile to the local seafood distributor. There, he was paid one cent per clam—the going rate in the early 1950s.

When I was ten, I spent my fourth consecutive summer with my grandparents and aunt in Hatteras. I will always appreciate them—and my parents—for allowing me to spend three months each year in such a perfect setting.

It's easy to forget that this was a Hatteras without paved roads, with no Oregon Inlet bridge, no motels, no tourists to speak of, no houses. At my grandparents' house, we had no electricity, no telephones, no television, and no indoor plumbing. The only source of potable water in the village was rain collected on rooftops and funneled through gutters into cisterns, a feature in every home.

Hatteras was a place with 60 miles of pristine shoreline and numerous shipwrecks that remained undisturbed except by nature. Its clean waters teemed with marine life. Life there was simple, relaxed, and characterized by a dialect that distinguished its people. Since Hatteras Island was geographically isolated for centuries, long stretches of barrier islands, separated from the mainland by sounds and inlets, meant little outside contact. Early settlers (1600s–1700s) were mainly from England's West Country, the British Isles, and parts of Scotland and Ireland, so their speech preserved certain Elizabethan English sounds and words that faded from other parts of the country. The traditional Outer Banks dialect—often called the "Hoi Toider" (High Tider) accent—has a unique phonetic feature. The "ai" sound shifts toward "oi."

For my brother and me, it was also a Hatteras free from the influence of our father. My father was an alcoholic—though when not plagued by his addiction, he worked to provide for his family, made sure we had a trustworthy car, and on occasion, accompanied us out to Hatteras. Although my mother missed us terribly during those long summers, she was willing to make that sacrifice so we could experience the stability of a loving home—even if only for a few months each year. It wasn't until I was much older that I understood the extent of her selflessness.

At ten years old, it was just how I lived: summers on a remote island, away from my parents, with grandparents and an aunt who loved me—and whom I loved as much as life itself. That summer, I went on my first clamming trip with Pop Pop, and I saw a sea cucumber for the first time.

As we left the house to go clamming, Grandmom followed Pop Pop and me out to the pizer. She performed her usual ritual—grabbing one of the porch posts, leaning forward, and peering toward the sound in the western sky. If there were any clouds, no matter how small, she would worry and start making excuses for why I should stay home. "It's going to come up a squall pretty soon, and you better not leave home," she would say. "Your mother particularly charged me to take good care of you, and it is unsafe for you to be outside or away from home during a thunder squall."

Grandmom had a deep fear of storms. Whenever I asked to play with neighborhood friends, she would glance anxiously at the sky for any hint of bad weather. Her worry over summer storms often kept me indoors longer than I liked. When a thunderstorm passed over the village, she gathered everyone into a room without a chimney, insisting that chimneys attracted lightning. We were told to sit quietly and stay silent until the storm passed. In that silence, the sounds of wind, rain, and thunder seemed louder. After every flash of lightning and its inevitable crack of thunder, I could always count on one of Grandmom's high-pitched screams. Sometimes, it was genuinely unnerving.

A few summer clouds drifted over the sound that morning, but I knew that no matter how much she begged or pleaded, Pop Pop would spare me from her storm edict. His response was always the same: "Now, Mag, go on back in the house and don't worry. We'll be all right. I'll take care of the boy."

"Clifford, you know his mother would be worried sick if she knew he was out in the sound with a storm a coming up. I am not going to be responsible if anything happens to him!" With that said and her conscience cleared, she went back inside, acting as if the whole world had turned against her.

It was a mile-long hike down a sandy, unpaved road to the shoreside where Pop Pop kept his skiff. The locals called that end of the village "Sticky Bottom" due to its predominant marshy topography. I was already tired by the time we passed the fish houses and docks in the village harbor—only halfway to the boat. Pop Pop told me we'd bring our clams back to the fish house at the end of the day to sell them.

After what felt like hours of walking through the deep, loose sand along the road, we finally reached the skiff. My granddaddy untied the boat, and with me already inside, pushed it from above the high-tide line down the embankment into the shallow waters of the sound.

For the first ten feet or so from the shoreline, in water too shallow for the boat to stay afloat, an abrasive sound resonated from the bottom of the skiff as it scraped along the sand. When the water deepened enough to float, the skiff's sudden, smooth glide gave me a feeling of freedom—a break from the

Pop Pop's skiff looked like the one in this painting by an unknown local artist.
(From author's collection)

drag of friction. The soft splashing of ripples against the hull was music to my ears. Even now, that sound forms for me a deep connection—both captivating and mysterious.

When Pop Pop stepped into the skiff, it suddenly rocked, and the water splashed more forcefully against its hull. With the balance of a tightrope walker, he made his way to the back of the boat.

Extending from the floor at the stern and resting across the front seat, a long pole stretched out over the bow. Pop Pop used it to push the skiff to our clamming spot, about a mile from shore. Standing on the raised platform at the stern, he planted the pole firmly on the sound's bottom and, with each push, turned his effort into steady forward motion.

I sat near the bow, gazing west into a cloudless sky, as a gentle southwesterly breeze brushed my face. My senses were flooded with images that etched themselves on my mind—still sharp after more than seventy years, like sunlit photographs.

I still see Pop Pop and me in his simple wooden skiff, peacefully gliding over shallow, sparkling, emerald-green waters. The sky was a brilliant blue, with the golden sun warming our backs. The warm, humid air carried the pungent smell of sulfur from the nearby salt marsh, but the scent faded as we drifted farther into the sound.

Shorebirds squawked—some diving or wading for food, others gliding above on invisible threads of wind. The shoreline gradually shifted eastward, as if the world itself was letting go. Even now, I find it hard to believe that heaven's streets of gold could match that quiet splendor.

With the anchor overboard to secure the skiff, Pop Pop stepped into two feet of water. I followed, and the water felt noticeably warmer than the ocean water where I'd been swimming the day before. The bottom was soft, made of fine, slightly oozy sand—less firm than the ocean floor. Patches of eelgrass appeared here and there, and I didn't enjoy wading through them barefoot; it made it harder to see what I might be stepping on. Though I had little fear of what lurked below, I preferred to see it before I stepped on it.

That slight discomfort turned into real anxiety when Pop Pop said, "Son, be careful and don't step on any stingrays." He explained that it wasn't un-common to find them half-buried in the sandy shallows, hunting clams—an essential part of their diet. He warned me that stepping on a stingray's back could lead to a painful sting. At that point, I began to think that clamming might not be quite as fun as I'd imagined.

Pop Pop set the two #2 zinc tubs from the skiff into the water beside us. Each floating tub had a short piece of rope—about five feet long—tied to its handle. He tied the other end of each rope around our waists. As we collected clams, we dropped them into the tubs, which bobbed behind us.

He handed me one of the two clam rakes at the bottom of the skiff and kept the other for himself. The rakes had unusually long, sharp-looking tines, with a wire net stretched between the handle's end and the crossbar where the tines were welded.

For a few minutes, Pop Pop taught me the art of clamming—how to push the rake along the sandy bottom, recognize the telltale scratching sound when a tine scraped a clam, and retrieve it by scooping and flipping the rake so the clam landed in the wire net.

I was eager—and determined—to dig up more clams than Pop Pop. Each one a small victory. I started clam-digging beside him, feeling safer from the stingrays there. Pushing the rake was tiring. For every clam I pulled up, Pop Pop brought in five. I quickly realized I couldn't keep up with him at that pace. I figured he had an advantage—he must have known precisely where to look.

Raking for clams on a shallow shoal near the Hatteras shoreline

Thinking I could outsmart him, I mistakenly moved ahead, hoping to find the clams before he did. But the sound of clams dropping into his tub kept coming steadily. How was he still finding so many in an area I had already raked?

His tub was already a third full, while mine barely had a layer on the bottom. The longer I clammed, the braver I became. Within a couple of hours, I was nearly 50 feet ahead, working as hard as I could to catch up. Still, he trailed behind me, effortlessly finding clams I had missed. I was often distracted by the many amazing critters that either got caught in the wire mesh of my clam rake or swam or crawled nearby. I kept asking Pop Pop, "What is this?" The more questions I asked, the further I fell behind in my mission to catch as many clams as he did.

My granddaddy was a prankster. He loved to horse around—wrestling, throwing playful punches, and stirring up mischief. More often than not, my brother and I were on the receiving end of his antics. We loved every second of it. Sometimes, we had to step back when he forgot his strength, but we always came back for more.

That day, when I wasn't paying attention, Pop Pop scooped up an unfamil-

Pop Pop mending a net

iar creature with his clam rake. In his younger days, Pop Pop played base-
ball, with pitching as his specialty. Using that skill, he drew back his right
arm, aimed, and threw the strange organism straight at the back of my head
with incredible speed. He couldn't have made a more perfect hit if he'd fired
it from a rifle with a scope.

I was carefully working the clam rake when a living missile struck the back
of my head. I had no idea what had hit me, but after the initial thud, I saw
stars and felt a quick, sharp jolt of pain. Instinctively, I lowered my chin to
my chest and saw an incredible sight. Entangled around my neck and draped

over my shoulders and chest were what looked like five or more feet of slender, milky-white intestines. They were slick, rubbery, and utterly repulsive.

I yelled out—startled both by the impact and by the slimy mass now on my upper body. I crouched in the water, frantically splashing and jumping to wash away the necklace of alien organic matter I had no desire to touch. Amid the chaos, I heard laughter behind me. That's when it clicked—Pop Pop was behind this. Even after I managed to scrub the strange guts from my body, he kept roaring with laughter.

Eventually, curiosity surpassed both my embarrassment and irritation. I quickly forgave Pop Pop for his prank and used my clam rake to retrieve the strange creature that had ricocheted off my head and fallen into the water.

What was this strange, cucumber-shaped creature that had spilled its repulsive entrails across my neck and chest? Pop Pop didn't have a name for it, and the mystery remained until that day in zoology class during my sophomore year of college.

CHAPTER 6

Going to Uncle Luther's

Many intriguing images come to mind when I think of Hatteras—shipwrecks are among them. As a young boy, while sitting at the surf's edge and gazing at the ocean, I tried to picture what the space occupied by the sea would look like if the water were gone. I envisioned myself walking among the hundreds of wrecks, collecting gold and jewels that had lain for centuries on the bottom of this Graveyard of the Atlantic.

In time, I discovered that the ocean did not possess all the nearby treasures alone. Hatteras Village had its share, too. Some such valuables were just across the sandy road from my grandparents' home.

Uncle Luther wasn't my real uncle. In our neighborhood in Hatteras, it was customary for kids to call men "uncle" and women "aunt." I considered Uncle Luther my actual uncle and Aunt Ellen, his wife, my true aunt. They were incredibly kind to me, so I seized every opportunity to be in their company. Grandmom was always protective and hesitant to let me wander far while I was under her care during my summer visit. Yet, despite her constant worry that something might happen to me, she made an exception for me to cross the road to visit them. She trusted them completely and believed I would be just as safe with them as I would be at home with her.

After Libby, the daughter of Uncle Luther and Aunt Ellen, married, she and her husband lived with her parents. During that time, Ted, their first grandson, was born. He was the cutest child. I have always loved caring for children, so going to Uncle Luther's to babysit Ted felt like a double reward.

Uncle Luther whittling, early 1950s

I could fulfill a fleeting paternal instinct by watching over an adorable kid. It was also a chance to learn some Hatteras history firsthand while visiting Uncle Luther in his woodworking shop.

During that particular summer, on weekday mornings around 9:30 a.m., when I didn't go swimming at the beach or exploring at the landing, I walked down the path from our house to the road, often dodging mud fiddlers that wandered in from the nearby marsh. I crossed the narrow road with its deep sand ruts and trudged barefoot to the back of Aunt Ellen and Uncle Luther's house through a sandy yard dotted with patches of pennywort.

Two steps at the end of a short walkway led up to their cement back porch, which spanned the entire width of the house. The porch floor was the top of a cistern that collected and stored rainwater from the roof. Fresh water was a limited resource in Hatteras during those days, and everyone practiced water conservation.

Directly across the porch from the steps was the back door leading into the kitchen. Many layers of paint covered the door, the most recent being light

Aunt Ellen and Uncle Luther and the violin, late 1950s

green. The lower half of the door was solid, with the upper frame covered by a screen. The screen was white, and dried paint obstructed some holes in the netting.

I was tall enough to peer through the screen netting into the kitchen, where nine-month-old Ted splashed about in the kitchen sink each day during his morning bath. Grandmom told me not to "track up their house," so without stepping inside, I greeted Ted's mom, backed away from the door, walked across the porch, and sat down in a swing suspended on long chains attached to the high porch ceiling.

It was an amazing old swing covered in numerous layers of the same light green paint as the back door. With every push, the long chains of the swing allowed it to travel in a long, graceful arc. The downward plunge brought a rush of weightlessness, only to be followed by the anticipation of the climb back up. Each ride was a heart-pounding blend of freedom and excitement, leaving me grinning and craving more.

After Ted was powdered and diapered, his mom carried him outside and placed him next to me in the swing. For the next half-hour, we experienced the joy and excitement of the swing's motion while his mom took a moment for herself. Ted smiled and giggled with each push of the swing. When it was time for his morning nap, his mother came out onto the porch and thanked me for keeping him entertained. As she carried him into the house, I told Ted to enjoy his nap and that I would see him the next day.

Before I left the porch surrounded by the comfortable, gentle southwesterly breeze, I couldn't resist taking a couple more swings. On the final forward arc, I slipped from the seat, allowing the inertia of my body to carry me through the air several feet across the porch. For a moment before landing on the cement floor, I felt as free as an osprey gliding on the wind currents in the deep blue morning sky of Hatteras.

Uncle Luther had two outbuildings behind his house. In one, he stored an endless supply of hunting, clamming, and fishing gear, while the other housed his car. The garage featured a small room attached to one side, with a bank of windows overlooking a ditch that ran alongside a tranquil salt marsh filled with lush green spartina and patches of needle rush. Here was where Uncle Luther set up his woodworking shop. The open windows caught the warm summer breeze, while Uncle Luther carved birds and built birdhouses. I always found him working there after Ted went inside for his morning nap.

"Morning, Uncle Luther," I said as I stood in the doorway from the garage into the shop.

"Hey, son, come on in and have a seat," he said with his usual welcoming smile. He gestured to an old church bench next to the wall.

Uncle Luther created ducks and geese from blocks of wood. He had various tools, and I was amazed at how skillfully he used them. I often thought that someday I would carve birds and build birdhouses like Uncle Luther. But what I enjoyed most during my visits were our conversations. Like my grandfather, he loved to talk about the old times, and I loved listening. All I had to do was ask the right questions and the adventures of the past would unfold.

"Uncle Luther, will you tell me about when you worked at the Gooseville Gun Club?"

"Sure, son. What do you want to know?"

"I want to know about that millionaire who came here and built it," I said, leaning back against the pew that once was a fixture in the first Methodist church in Hatteras Village.

"You mean Mr. Albert Lyon?" he asked, looking up from the cypress block

Uncle Luther's carved gull

that would become another of the many seagulls he carved, painted, and sold to tourists.

"Yes, sir. How did he know about Hatt'ras?"

Hatteras was a three-syllable word for those who live off the island; to the locals, it was simply two.

Old man Lyon first came to Hatteras with Rex Beach, a sportsman and writer, on Beach's houseboat. She was a fine boat fully equipped for hunting. She had everything on her a hunter would need to kill wild fowl. Old man Lyon enjoyed hunting here so much that he bought a 1,500-acre tract of land from my brother Andrew that stretched from the southern end of the village all the way to Hatteras Inlet. In 1927, he built the Gooseville Gun Club. My younger brother, Ernest, was hired as the caretaker."

Uncle Luther glanced up from his carving and looked out the window toward his brother Ernest's house, which swas visible on the south side of the salt marsh.

"I thought you were the caretaker," I said,

"Oh, I was," he quickly replied. "Ernest was only there for a few years before he died. Died of a brain tumor. Old man Lyon hired me right after that."

Uncle Luther paused, driving his knife deep into the cypress block, starting the shaping of the gull's neck and head.

With a bit of mist in his eye, he added, "Ernest thought so much of old man Lyon that he named his youngest son, Bert, after him."

Even at a young age, I sensed Uncle Luther's sadness as he spoke about his deceased brother. I gently shifted the subject by asking, "How did Mr. Lyon become so rich?"

"Why son, he invented the bumper of the automobile," he replied with pride. "Not only invented it but manufactured them too."

"Gosh, he must have been mighty rich," I said.

"He was. He invented lots of stuff, and it made him a millionaire. You should have seen the guns he owned. Why, he had all kinds of guns at the Club. He had several old army guns. Automatics. One type of gun there had three barrels."

"Three barrels?"

"Yes sir, three barrels. If you put one bullet in her, she shot just one. If you put two bullets in her, she'd shoot two. And if you wanted to shoot three bullets at once, then you loaded all three barrels. Why one of his hunting buddies even had a gun with a solid gold trigger."

"Dag on, he must have been rich too," I said.

"Imagine so," Uncle Luther said as the cypress gull's head began to take shape.

"Whereabouts did they hunt?" I asked.

"Mostly out on the reef in the sound. They done some hunting on the land but mostly on the reef. I've set out many of a boatload of decoys on the reef where they killed geese, ducks, and brant. The ducks and brant were so plentiful that when they came up out of the marsh, it looked like a cloud was a rising. And on a calm night, boys-o-man, they made so much racket that you couldn't sleep."

"Why ain't they thick like that today?"

"The grass they liked to eat got some kind of a disease. As the grass died out so did the fowl. And thousands of the birds was killed during World War II. What I mean is, when ships and submarines were destroyed and sunk just offshore here, there was a lot of oil that got in the water. Many times I saw

The Gooseville Gun Club duck

hundreds of birds die from their feathers being gummed up in the oil. Sometimes we'd go along the shoreside and shoot them to keep them from suffering. Things never did get right after that."

Uncle Luther paused, staring at the gull he was carving. He gently shook his head from side to side, pressing his lips tightly over his teeth. I understood what he was thinking about: his love for what Hatteras once was and his regret that it would never be that way again.

He got up and walked to a corner of his shop filled with a small pile of decoys. "These here cedar decoys is the kind I was talking about," he said as he reached down and picked one up. He passed it to me. "This is the last one left from the old Club."

"She is a beauty," I said as I turned the wooden duck around. I put the bird close to my nose and sniffed its crisp, clean cedar odor. GOOSEVILLE GUN CLUB was branded on its bottom. I felt as if I were holding a treasure as valuable as any that the nearby sea had to offer.

"Would you like to have it?" Uncle Luther asked.

I could not believe my ears. "Would I like to have it? Why you bet!" With my next breath, I said, "I know exactly what I will do with it. It is going to go on a shelf in my bedroom. Uncle Luther, I'll keep this forever."

"You do that, son," he replied, patting my head as if to say you're welcome. Then he said, "Come to think of it, I made a similar vow to a good friend of mine . . . Tom Angell."

"Oh yeah, I heard Mama talking about him. She said that when she was a little girl growing up here at Hatt'ras, everyone loved going to Tom's house

Tom Angell, early 1930s

on Sundays to eat his homemade ice cream and chocolate cake. Wasn't he the only colored man that ever lived on Hatt'ras?" I asked.

"He sure was," replied Uncle Luther.

"So, how did you and Tom get to be friends?"

"We worked together at the Gooseville Gun Club. Tom was the cook. Tom and me, we took a lot of pride in making sure everybody had a good visit when old man Lyon and his friends came down here from Detroit to go hunting and fishing. Tom, he sure cooked some good meals. Tom and me got to be real good friends. They won't nothing that one of us would not do for the other."

"If Tom was the first colored man to live down here, where did he come from?"

"It seems that this feller named Nelson Angell and his wife moved here from Boston to run the Oliver Reef Lighthouse. It was located in Pamlico Sound, about five miles from the harbor here at Hatt'ras. While on a trip to New Bern in 1869, Mrs. Angell saw this little seven-year-old colored boy named Tom Vine wandering up and down the streets. She thought he looked neglected, so she found his mother and asked her if she could adopt him. His

Angell house

mother agreed. The Angells brought him to Hatt'ras and taught him to help with chores around the house." As he spoke, Uncle Luther kept shaping the gull's head from the cypress block.

"Tom was a faithful worker for the Angells, who gained the respect of the people of Hatt'ras. Everyone had only good things to say about him. One day, Tom asked Mrs. Angell if he could change his last name to Angell. She agreed, saying it would be all right so long as he didn't disgrace the family name. Old man Angell's death was followed shortly by Mrs. Angell's passing away in 1911. She gave Tom a life estate in her Hatteras home, which she had designed and built. Until his death, twenty-six years later, Tom lived in the house and kept it just like Mrs. Angell left it."

Uncle Luther reached into his pocket and pulled out a plug of Apple chewing tobacco. He used his carving knife to slice a piece from the plug and place it in his mouth. After several chews, he continued.

"Tom enjoyed music. He had an organ and a banjo. He tried to play them, but he won't very good at it."

"My mama said he had a beautiful voice," I said. "She told me when she was a little girl, she heard him singing in church, and it sounded like the angels themselves were singing there." We both chuckled—an Angell singing like an angel.

Uncle Luther continued, "It seems that this Swede who worked on the Diamond Shoals Lightship had this violin. He brought it ashore several times and played it at dances they held out on the beach. Tom thought it had the most beautiful sound, and he asked if he could buy it. The Swede refused to sell it to Tom, and later, he sold it to a feller named Iris Willis, one of the boys from down here."

Uncle Luther stood up and walked to the nearest open window of the shop. He leaned out, spat a stream of brown tobacco juice into the ditch below, and wiped his mouth on his right sleeve. On returning to his seat, Uncle Luther examined the wingless body of the seagull at arm's length and eye level. He looked at the cypress bird first from its side and then from the front. Once he was satisfied that its body parts were proportional, he placed the bird on the table in front of him.

"All that's left to do is the wings," he said.

"Why didn't the Swede sell the violin to Tom?" I asked.

"I don't know," said Uncle Luther, "but Tom finally did get it. It seems that Iris Willis got into some trouble with the law for mommocking a horse. He needed money to leave town to keep from getting arrested, so he sold the violin to Tom."

"Mommocking" is our word we used to mean "abusing."

Uncle Luther picked up a thin piece of cypress that was lying near his foot on the floor. "This will work," he said. I sat captivated watching the work of a master carver using his knife to shape a pair of wings.

"Could Tom play the violin?" I inquired.

"No, but others did when he carried it out to Ellsworth Balance's pavilion on the beach, where they had square dances on Saturday nights. She was played so much that her pegs wore slam out. Tom had to order some new ones for her from Sears and Roebuck. That violin had the most beautiful tone. A lot of people around here remarked about that," said Uncle Luther as a piece of shaving from the cypress scrap that he was carving flew into my lap. "Hey, those wood shavings have a mind of they own, don't they?" laughed Uncle Luther.

After a couple of chuckles, he continued, "When Tom was taken sick just before he died, Dr. Kenfield went to Tom's house to doctor him. He noticed the violin lying on Mrs. Angell's old sideboard. Dr. Kenfield picked it up to

Uncle Luther's violin

examine it and noticed a date inside it. He told Tom that it must be over one hundred years old. No one around here had ever noticed a date in her before."

"What was the date in it?" I asked.

"I don't know that I ever paid any attention to it," replied Uncle Luther.

He finished the first wing and held it next to the right side of the wingless gull's body. He picked up a nail from the bench in front of him and scratched a spot on the gull's body where the wing would be attached. He cut a shallow groove in the body where the base of the wing would be inserted and glued.

As he began carving the left wing, he resumed his story.

"Tom sent for me when he knew he was going to die. He said he wanted me to see after him on his deathbed and to make sure that all his bills was paid. The day before his death, Tom got out the violin and told me to take it home. He said that back a long time ago, he remembered me telling him that I'd love to have a violin like his. He said, 'Now you have one, and I want you to take good care of it.'"

Suddenly, Uncle Luther stopped midsentence and paused his carving, his sharp eyes locking onto the greenhead fly that had dared to land on his arm. Determined to thwart the sting, he precisely swung his hand, delivering a swift, fatal blow that sent the fly tumbling to the shop floor. Without hesitation, Uncle Luther drove the worn, crepe rubber sole of his blue canvas slip-on shoe down onto the insect.

"Do you still have the violin?" I eagerly wanted to know.

"I sure do. Let me finish up this here wing, and I'll show her to you."

My heart started thumping in anticipation of seeing the old violin. I could not recall ever having seen anything over a hundred years old.

After Uncle Luther applied glue to the wings and inserted them into the grooves on the side of the gull's body, he led me from the shop and into his kitchen.

He opened the closet door where Aunt Ellen stored brooms, mops, an ironing board, and other household items. He reached up for the violin on a high shelf in the closet.

He carefully passed it to me, saying, "I think the world of this old violin. When he gave her to me, I told Tom that I would keep her for the rest of my life, and so far, I have. I don't know what she is worth since she is so old and all, but she is priceless to me because a dear friend gave her to me."

As a college student a decade later, I asked Uncle Luther if I could take another look at the violin. It was still on the top shelf of the closet in the kitchen. I peeked through the fancy cut openings on the face of the violin, searching for the date that Dr. Kenfield had noted a few weeks before Tom died in 1937. I could hardly believe what I saw. Dr. Kenfield was right; the violin was over one hundred years old. If what I was reading was not a mistake, it was closer to two hundred years old! The last two digits of the date were challenging to read, but the first two numbers, one and seven, were clear. Someone had also written a person's name, town, and country in faded ink. My heart began to race, much like when I first saw the violin. Time has erased the inscription of the person's name from my memory, but Cremona, Italy, was the town and country. I jotted down all the information I found on a crumpled piece of paper I had stuffed in my wallet.

When I returned to college, I headed straight to the library, my curiosity burning. I dove into the search, and to my astonishment, I didn't have to look far. There it was—a name tied to history itself! It belonged to an apprentice of the legendary Antonio Stradivari. He had lived and worked in Cremona, Italy, during the very era marked inside the violin. I could hardly believe it—one of the greatest names in musical history had a connection to the instrument I held!

The next time I saw Uncle Luther, I shared my discovery with him, but he was not impressed. Stradivarius meant nothing to him. What mattered most was that his friend Tom had honored him by entrusting him with the care of his most prized possession. Uncle Luther continued to celebrate that friendship until he passed away, nurturing a violin he couldn't play.

I understand how Uncle Luther felt, for I have also been honored to own two treasures. My dear friend, Uncle Luther, gave both of them to me. One is a valuable duck decoy from the Gooseville Gun Club that I have kept prominently in my home for over seventy years. The other is the seagull Uncle Luther carved the morning he showed me the violin.

CHAPTER 7

Going to Get Religion

During my younger years, spending summers in Hatteras, Sunday was not just a day of rest but was also marked by restrictions, contrasts, conflicts, enlightenment, and gratitude toward God for everything. Someone was constantly reminding me that Sunday was God's day. I was certain God had appointed Grandmom to oversee His day, making sure that no one in the family did anything inappropriate. I often resented the attention He received throughout the day because it got in the way of what I wanted to do. I tried not to hold onto that resentment for too long because I feared God would condemn me to Hell. I learned a lot about Hell from Sunday school and revivals at the "Down Below" Pentecostal Holiness church. I learned about Heaven at the Methodist church in the village, although they also discussed Hell, but less often.

"Down Below" was the local name for the southern end of Hatteras Village, another name for Sticky Bottom, where Pop Pop had his clamming skiff. He and Grandmom grew up in Sticky Bottom. They began their married life there, where their children, my aunt Essie and my mother Naomi, were born. After their parents passed away, Grandmom and Pop Pop decided to move up the road because Grandmom wanted to be closer to her only surviving sister. They bought a house and four acres of land for four hundred dollars on the main road directly across from Grandmom's sister, Aunt Katie.

Before the early 1950s, Hatteras Village had only two roads, both of which were unpaved. Locals referred to the front road, a sandy lane on the village's

Line drawing of the original Methodist church in Hatteras

western side near the sound, and the back road, a similar path on the eastern ocean side. These roads ran parallel to each other and extended roughly in a north/south direction. Aunt Violet, who lived across the street from my grandparents, decided the roads and paths needed proper names. Unofficially, she named them after shipwrecks, historical markers, and local family surnames like Kohler Drive, Old Lighthouse Road, and Midgett Way. This is an example of how the locals didn't wait for outsiders to dictate things like road names, they just did it themselves. When the Department of Transportation took over the roads' maintenance, the names stuck. Even today, residents describe their location in the village as either up or down the road from some landmark. Thus, "up the road" and "down the road" are relative. "Up the road" indicates a spot to the north of any given landmark, while "down the road" refers to a point to the south.

Before moving, Grandmom and Pop Pop attended the "Down Below" church at Sticky Bottom, which was just across the marsh from their home. After relocating up the road, they joined the Methodist church closer to their house. They went regularly for a while but eventually stopped. Mama told me Grandmom felt her clothes weren't nice enough for the Methodist church. She said someone made fun of her frock one Sunday, which was her last visit. She never felt self-conscious about her attire at the church "Down Below." However, since walking was her only means of transportation, the "Down Below" church became too far to go. The only time I ever saw Grandmom in a house of worship was at her funeral in the Methodist church. I saw Pop Pop there twice: once at Grandmom's funeral and then at his own. Nevertheless, that doesn't mean they were not religious.

When electricity arrived in the village in the late '40s, Mama gifted Pop Pop a radio for Christmas. From that point on, every Sunday morning, he tuned in to his favorite station to hear some preaching. The gospel music blaring up the stairwell into my bedroom woke me every Sunday. The preacher on the radio was in high gear every time I came downstairs for breakfast. I never understood a word he said. To me, the preacher yelled indistinguishable words and phrases while constantly being interrupted by a barrage of amens and hallelujahs from his overly enthusiastic congregation. Pop Pop sat in his wooden rocking chair in the sitting room next to his radio, glued to every word the preacher spoke. He was so attentive that I had no doubt he understood every spoken word. I assumed that as I got older, I would be able to understand too. But that wasn't the case. In the years that followed, amen and hallelujah were all I grasped from the preacher. I wondered, "How could anyone comprehend what was being said with all the yelling?" I finally decided that Pop Pop didn't understand either. It was the atmosphere of the service that helped him focus on God.

For Grandmom, Sundays were just like any other day when it came to being attentive to the word of God. She read her Bible every evening after dinner. I will never forget how impressed I was by her religious perseverance when she finished the last chapter of Revelation one day, closed her Bible, and said, "That makes twenty-one times I've read this book from cover to cover." I could hardly believe my ears. How could anyone read a book that thick twenty-one times? I struggled to concentrate after reading just a few verses. I concluded she had to be the most religious person in the world, not only because of the number of times she had studied the "Word" but also due to the many rules that God had established. For instance, if you even used scissors on Sunday, you'd end up in the "bad place." She referred to Hell as the "bad place" when speaking to children.

No one could enjoy activities on Sunday without risking eternal damnation. Sitting on the pizer or visiting relatives on Sunday afternoons were the safest activities. My brother and I would occasionally persuade Sister, our Aunt Essie, to take us to the beach for a quick swim. Grandmom disapproved, but not forcefully. This leniency led me to believe there was some confusion in the Bible regarding how sinful it was to swim on a Sunday. She was so strict about observing the Sabbath as a day of rest that she prepared her Sunday dinner on Saturday afternoon. That way, all she had to do was heat the food before serving it after Sister returned from church. For supper that evening, we always had cold leftovers. There must have been some rule in the Bible about using a stove only once on Sunday.

After breakfast, my brother and I put on our Sunday clothes. We always wore a "starched and ironed" shirt, long pants, socks, and shoes. Sister gave each of us a nickel and some pennies to place on the offering plate. An offering was collected twice: once at the beginning of Sunday school and again when everyone gathered in the sanctuary to hear the preaching. I never knew if God wanted me to give the nickel in the sanctuary or in my class. As we assembled in the sanctuary for worship, I put my nickel on the wooden plate and reluctantly watched it vanish down the pew. I wanted to keep it, but guilt forced my hand. On Monday, my carefree brother used the nickel he had saved to buy candy at the local store.

My Aunt Essie, my mother's sister who never married and lived with her parents all her life, took her weekly bath on Sunday mornings in her bedroom. Since we didn't have indoor plumbing, she filled a ceramic washbowl with water and carried it upstairs to her room. She emerged a half-hour later, smelling as fresh as the ocean breeze. She used Avon dusting powder, which I always associate with Sunday mornings. Her only makeup was Noxzema Skin Cream and lipstick. For most of my childhood, her only Sunday dress was a light blue and white striped skirt with a matching jacket and a white

The Methodist church in the early 1950s

blouse. She wore nylon stockings and white slip-on shoes with low heels. In her small purse was some change, which she donated to the church when the offering was collected. Also in the bag was half a stick of gum, just in case she needed to freshen her breath between Sunday school and church. She was a soft-spoken, nonjudgmental person who saw only the good in everyone she knew. As she descended the steps from her bedroom, squeaky clean and dressed in her Sunday best, she was as close to being an angel as any human.

Fifteen minutes before Sunday school started, Damon Junior rang the church bell. Everyone in the village who attended took this as their cue to start the walk to church. My aunt, my brother, and I walked together. As we left the house and reached the sandy road, we encountered Aunt Maude, Aunt Ellen, and Aunt Violet, who were also on their way to church. They weren't related to me, but everyone was an "Aunt" or "Uncle" in our neighborhood.

Like Pop Pop, none of the men in the neighborhood went to Sunday school or church; interestingly, very few men in the whole village did. I often wondered why religion felt more significant to women than to men. Many of the children attended Sunday school, but not always church services. My brother and I only went to Sunday school, while Sister stayed for church.

As we arrived at the church, so did everyone else. Sunday was the only day of the week when many people walked along the road from all directions. Before entering, all the women paused at the front door. Leaning one hand against the door frame for balance, they emptied the sand from their shoes with the other. Everyone's shoes got filled with sand from the deep ruts of fine sand that formed the paths around the village. No sooner was everyone inside the sanctuary than Damon Junior tugged the rope attached to the steeple's bell. Several chimes signaled the start of Sunday school.

Each family member sat in the same pews every Sunday. Mr. Roy Gray, the superintendent of Sunday school, stepped before the congregation. His deep, baritone voice echoed through the church walls, producing a pleasing, steady resonance that sounded like God himself. After making a few announcements, he asked us to turn to hymn number 145 in our hymnbooks. Damon Junior's wife, Miss Alice, always played the piano barefoot or in her stocking feet. Once she played several introductory chords, the congregation would joyfully sing "The Old Rugged Cross," often followed by another beautiful hymn like "Bringing in the Sheaves." The congregation's voices drifted from the open windows of the church, enveloping the village in the presence of God. Hearing those hymns sung in the local dialect brought a lump to my throat and tears of joy to my eyes. It is sound that no longer exists. With today's influx of tourists, radio, television, and other outside influences, the old Hatteras dialect, the result of many years of isolation from the mainland, is all but extinct.

I remember on one particular Sunday—I must have been in my early teens—after the offering plates were passed, Mr. Roy asked if anyone had celebrated a birthday in the past week. Miss Inez, an older lady in the community, and Ursula, a friend, proudly walked to the front of the church with their birthday offerings, contributing a penny for each year since their birth. After everyone sang "Happy Birthday," Mr. Roy read a passage from the Bible, and we sang another hymn. Then he dismissed us to our Sunday school classroom.

Miss Lizzy, a rather stern conservative lady in her early seventies, taught my brother's class. Clifford and Miss Lizzy were like oil and water. Nothing my brother did ever pleased her, and the feeling was mutual for him.

Their enmity had begun one afternoon when Clifford played among the branches of an oak tree in front of Aunt Violet's house. He hid on a limb that overhung the road, waiting for an unsuspecting passerby. Miss Lizzy was walking up the road from the grocery store to her home. As she passed beneath him, he dropped a device with an explosive cap at her feet. The sharp crack startled her so much that she flung her bag of groceries into the air. Her reaction sent jars and food items scattering all over the road. Even those living on the "back road" heard her scream.

It never occurred to Clifford that she might react this way. He believed they would both share a good laugh, and the incident would soon be forgotten. When she spotted Clifford, who was now a bit embarrassed and frightened, clinging to the branch above the road, her shock turned to anger. Clifford understood as soon as the cap exploded that his action was misguided, but it was too late. His only defense was a flat-out denial, insisting he had never seen the device that now lay at Miss Lizzy's feet. His lie only intensified her volatile state. From that moment on, they became adversaries.

Miss Lizzy started her Sunday school lesson that day by reading passages from Genesis about Noah and the ark. When she reached the part about Noah being five hundred years old when he "begat" his three sons, Clifford challenged her.

"Are you sure he was that old?"

"Why, of course, it says so right here in the Bible," she responded as she pointed to the passage in Genesis 5, verse 32.

"Well, I ain't never heard of anyone living that long," Clifford stated.

Miss Lizzy continued her story, only to be interrupted again when she read about the ark made from gopherwood.

"What is gopherwood?" asked Clifford.

Unsure but not wanting to seem uninformed, she replied, "It's a special kind of wood."

"Well, I've heard of pine, hickory, walnut, and mahogany, but I've never heard of gopherwood. Nobody around here has a boat made of gopherwood, does he? Are you sure you read that right?"

"Yes, I did. It says gopherwood right here in Genesis 6, verse 14." Again, she pointed to the passage as the other kids giggled, impatience starting to flow through her veins.

When she told the children about the animals being brought onto the ark two by two, Clifford interrupted again. Laying the groundwork for Miss Lizzy's upcoming inquiry, he asked, "Where do polar bears live?"

She answered, "At the North Pole," without realizing where Clifford's questioning might lead.

"Were there polar bears on the ark?"

"Yes, he put two of every kind of animal on the ark."

"Did he go to the North Pole to get the polar bears?"

"I suppose so."

"How far is it from the Holy Land to the North Pole?"

"Oh, I don't know—a long way."

"How long did it take him to go there, catch the polar bears, and return to the ark?" Miss Lizzy pretended she did not hear him and continued with her lesson.

Again, her challenger interrupted, "Miss Lizzy, did he have any kangaroos on the ark?"

"Certainly, I told you he had two of every animal."

"Where did he get the kangaroos from?"

"I suppose from somewhere nearby."

"I thought kangaroos only lived in Australia. Is the Holy Land near Australia?"

"No, Australia is an island continent between the Pacific and Indian Oceans. The Holy Land is a way from there," Miss Lizzy proudly stated. Her expression reflected a hint of pride because she finally had an undeniable answer to one of his questions.

"Then where did he get the kangaroos?" Clifford demanded.

The snickering in class ceased as the kids sat puzzled, eager to discover where Noah had acquired those kangaroos. He had backed Miss Lizzy into a corner, and she was aware of it. Questioning anything in the Bible never crossed her mind; she simply accepted it.

"You should not question the word of God," she firmly stated, shaking her finger at Clifford while piercing him with her seething gaze.

In a feeble attempt to seem somewhat knowledgeable about Clifford's question, she added, "But there are kangaroos all over. They are in zoos right here in this country. I'm sure Noah had no trouble finding them where he was."

And on with the lesson, she talked about Noah being six hundred years old and that God told him to build the ark. She also mentioned the rain lasting forty days and forty nights and how the ark floated for 150 days after the rain stopped. Without pausing for breath, she lectured on how Noah sent out a raven followed by a dove in search of land, the dove returning with the olive leaf, and finally about letting the animals out of the ark to "go forth and multiply."

At this point, Clifford chuckled, "I bet that was one stinking ark."

The kids howled, to Clifford's delight.

When Miss Lizzy regained control of the class, she concluded her lesson by reading Genesis 8:20. "And Noah built an altar, and took of every beast and fowl, and offered burnt offerings on the altar."

"After being shut up on that ark for 190 days or more, I'll bet he had trouble finding any clean beasts or fowl," Clifford said.

The class erupted in laughter. When the laughter finally died down, Clifford posed his last question just before the teacher dismissed them. "It seems mighty strange to me that after going to all that trouble to collect those animals and keep them on the ark for over 190 days, he would then turn around and burn some of them as an offering."

He paused as the neurons in his brain fired, leading to his final thought, which he expressed as if he were on the verge of a brilliant discovery. "Is that why there are no dinosaurs living today? Noah used them as a sacrifice?"

The kids in the class glanced at one another and then back at Miss Lizzy, seeking an answer. A brief silence followed. Slowly, her expression took on an air of elation that often accompanies the discovery of a profound truth. She replied with confidence, "Ab-so-lutely!"

Sunday school at the Holiness church started at 2:00 p.m. There was just enough time after dinner to walk the long distance down the road to the church and arrive before the service began. It was a long, hot walk from our house along the sandy road. The sand's texture was extremely fine. With each step, our feet sank deeply into the powdery surface. It felt as if we were trudging through quicksand, making it exhausting. We were completely soaked in sweat by the time we reached the church.

The Holiness church presented many contrasts to the one we had attended just a few hours earlier. In comparison to the larger Methodist church, this one was a small, simple-framed building with only two classrooms adjacent to the sanctuary. Another difference was that the women attending the Holiness church dressed much more plainly and wore their hair straight, typically styled into a bun at the back of their heads. They did not wear lipstick or rouge. They generally weighed more than the Methodist women and sweated considerably more. Most of them carried a clean white handkerchief in their right hand. Although more men attended this church, the women still outnumbered them. Most of the congregation lived at Sticky Bottom.

While the Methodist church exuded a gentle spirit, the Holiness church sometimes had a completely different atmosphere. Miss Alice never pounded the piano keys at the Methodist church like the lady who accompanied us as we sang hymns that afternoon. She struck the keys so forcefully that the floor gave way at one point, swallowing the right back leg of the piano and causing it to teeter like a seesaw. It must have been an act inspired by God because the preacher became wild, throwing his hands in the air and yelling, "Thank you-ah, God-ah! Hallelujah! Praise His holy name-ah!"

There was also something else that differed between the two churches: Mr. Roy at the Methodist church spoke English, while Reverend Culp spoke a variation of English that resembled Pig Latin. Mama taught me Pig Latin, but the more I listened to Reverend Culp, the more I realized it must have been some other form of Latin. I knew Catholics used Latin during worship because my cousins attended Catholic school and told me they heard one of the sisters speaking it.

Everyone at the Methodist church remained seated throughout the entire morning service. However, the Holiness folks had just as much trouble staying in their seats as my younger brother did in elementary school. Whenever the preacher began speaking in whatever Latin he used, the congregation jumped up from their seats, waved their hands, and started shouting. Each word ended with an extra syllable . . . ah. When the women sat back down, the long wooden pews snapped and cracked under the sudden weight they had to bear. However, it turned out that they were much stronger than the floor under the piano.

As best as I could interpret, Reverend Culp's sermon was that all of us would burn in Hell if we didn't change our evil ways. His subject certainly matched the temperature of the afternoon. It must have been one hundred degrees inside the small, crowded sanctuary. Midway through the service, I realized why the women weren't wearing makeup. Wearing makeup would have been a waste of money since their perspiration would have washed it away.

With each passing moment, the congregation became increasingly energetic and fervently enthusiastic. Many parishioners shouted "Hallelujah!" at the top of their lungs as they jumped up and down in their pews. It felt more like chaos than a place of worship. I found the whole scene unsettling.

The church windows were open to relieve the heat, allowing an occasional breeze to flow in from the ocean. There were no screens on the windows to keep out mosquitoes. During one of the rare quiet moments, Miss Liza, one of the larger parishioners who wheezed with each breath, accidentally inhaled a mosquito. This incident triggered an uncontrollable coughing fit. It affected her so violently that her neck muscles began to convulse, making it especially difficult for her to breathe. In a frantic attempt to catch her breath, she jumped from her seat, clutching her throat with one hand while waving the other in the air, crying out at the top of her lungs, "Help me, Jesus-ah." Reverend Culp interpreted her actions as inspired by the Holy Spirit. The lady at the piano started playing "Lord, I'm Coming Home." The congregation sang the hymn so loudly that people could hear it all over Sticky Bottom. Only Miss Liza and a few others sitting nearby understood how fitting that hymn was at the time. At the end of the service, Miss Liza gave a heart-wrenching testimony of how she had stared death in the face and survived. She delivered her testimony in the same Latin that Reverend Culp used throughout his sermons.

As I lay in bed that Sunday night, I prayed for God to bless Grandmom, Pop Pop, Sister, Mama, Aunt Katie, Aunt Violet, Aunt Ellen, Aunt Maude, Mr. Roy, Damon Junior, Miss Alice, Miss Inez, Ursula, Miss Lizzy, Miss Liza, and Reverend Culp. I asked Him to bless my brother, Clifford, Noah, and all the animals on the ark. I also asked Him to bless the people who lived down the road at Sticky Bottom and those who lived up the road where we lived. I thanked God for Hatteras, where I learned so much about life. I pleaded with God to send me a sign, like the rainbow He sent Noah, if Miss Lizzy was telling the truth about the extinction of the dinosaurs.

CHAPTER 8

Going to the Beach

And of course, remembering all those Hatteras summers, it's impossible not to remember my time on the beach itself. Who hasn't dreamed of stretching out on a deserted beach, untouched by any sign of human presence?

Fortunately for me, this was not a dream but was the beach I enjoyed for every summer of my childhood—and beyond.

A place where the dunes are scattered randomly instead of in perfect rows, with sea oats swaying gently in a light easterly breeze. On the sheltered side of the dunes, plants such as croton and seaside evening primrose flourish, protected from the ocean's salt spray. In contrast, on the ocean-facing side, more salt-tolerant, low-growing plants such as sea rocket and sea elder thrive.

A place where the berm is free of tire tracks. There is only beautiful golden sand shaped by wind and water from the high tide line to the base of the dunes. Occasionally, ghost crabs camouflaged against the sand scurry from furrow to furrow, while at night they scavenge for any organic matter.

A place where the gentle tides rise and fall, creating a zone of intertidal activity. Between the sand grains, microscopic creatures coexist alongside larger ones, such as mole crabs and clams.

A place where offshore energy moves toward the shore, manifesting as waves that lightly spill onto the beach.

A place where the summer sun infuses the entire ecosystem with vital energy.

A place where the only footprints from the dunes to the ocean's edge are yours. And as far as one can see, not another person is in sight.

The beach at Hatteras

Hatteras Village offered plenty of entertainment for my brother and me. There was fishing, clamming, hanging out at the docks, visiting relatives, and going to the movies at the picture show on Saturday night. Swimming at the beach wasn't a daily activity, but it was definitely something we looked forward to. We usually made our way to the beach on a weekday, accompanied by our Aunt Sister, unless one of our adult neighbors invited us to join them.

Sister had a midmorning break from her job, from 10:00 to 1:00. She'd already worked as a cashier at Mr. Dolph's store since 7:00, so the pause gave her a welcome recess before returning in the afternoon. Once or twice a week, this was our time for the beach. Clifford and I would be anxiously waiting in our bathing suits when she came home, as we were eager to jump in the ocean but dreading the long walk to get there. Sister never owned a bathing suit herself. Instead, she wore a tattered blouse with no sleeves, knee-length shorts, and a pair of sandals, while Clifford and I went barefoot.

With only sand roads the entire way, the walk to the beach seemed to take an eternity. The village of Hatteras was established on the sound side of the island. No one lived on the ocean side. The early settlers realized the foolishness of building on the beach. In today's world, where homes are constructed so close to the ocean, ignoring the wisdom of the settlers is a lesson learned the hard way. To get to the beach meant a walk through the village, followed by a trudge through coarse, deep sand for about half a mile to reach the cool water of the Atlantic.

I was already getting tired by the time we passed Mr. Dolph's store. My

Sister, Essie Mae Wade, on the beach at Hatteras

brother and I found that walking on the packed sand, following the ruts left by cars, was the easiest way to navigate through the sand. Since only a few people had cars, nearly everyone traveled around the village on foot. Onward we trudged, passing Mr. Ander's store, the movie theater, and the Methodist parsonage on our left and the old schoolhouse, Methodist church, and the girls' club on the right before crossing the old wooden bridge over Slash Creek. We passed several homes for the next quarter of a mile before arriving at the Atlantic View Hotel on our right. Built in 1928, it was the first hotel on

The Atlantic View Hotel

Hatteras Island. It mainly catered to sport fishermen, hunters, and occasional tourists. In the 1940s, a renovation doubled the original size of this historic structure. It had about 15 rooms and two bathrooms to accommodate guests who paid $1.50 per night, which included breakfast, dinner, and supper. It was the first building in Hatteras Village to have electricity.

Just beyond the hotel lay the straight path to the beach—the final stretch that always tested our determination to keep going. By this time, the heavy summer heat seemed to drain the last of our strength. Yet, just over the dunes, the promise of the Atlantic's cool water pulled us onward, giving us just enough courage to complete the trek. The sun pressed down on our shoulders. Each step felt slower. The sand was coarse and deep. Careful to sidestep the ever-present prickly pear cactus and tangles of catbrier, we finally reached the top of the dune. Spread out before us was a scene of pure serenity—a golden stretch of beach, soft, rhythmic waves creating a hissing sound as they gently rolled up the shore and beyond the emerald-green waters, whose ripples reflected dancing rays of sunlight sparkling like diamonds on an ocean that stretched three thousand miles beyond the horizon. What a breathtaking sight! Even now, after many years of going to the beach, I stand in awe, taking in the splendor of the familiar scene before me.

Me (with a new haircut) and Clifford enjoying the
beach in the early 1950s

My brother and I raced down the dune and onto the beach. It didn't take us long to jump in the surf, which produced a grin on our faces that lasted the entire stay. We didn't need any beach toys, chairs, or towels for creature comforts. We played in the surf and "air dried" when we came out of the water. Sister sat on the shoreside watching our every move, ready to correct us for overstepping our safety boundaries.

When we weren't body surfing or just splashing around, we kept ourselves busy digging with our hands in the intertidal zone for mole crabs and coquina clams. Mole crabs (also known as sand crabs of the genus Emerita) are small, oval-shaped crustaceans that live beneath the wet sand of the surf. Interestingly, they burrow backward in the sand when a wave washes over them, raising their antennae above the sand surface to filter water for plankton. Coquina clams (Donax variabilis) are small, wedge-shaped bivalves (two shells) that dwell in the shifting sands. Their shells are smooth, delicate, and brightly colored. When a wave rolls over them, they quickly bury themselves, feeding on plankton and organic matter they siphon from the water. After catching them, we marveled at how swiftly they vanished into the wet sand, wriggling beneath the surface almost the instant we set them down.

Bird watching was just as entertaining as sandpipers darted to the surf on tiny legs, where the incoming waves washed mole crabs and other small crustaceans to the surface, providing a fresh meal for the birds. We were amazed by how quickly and precisely these birds could peck their prey from the sand. While that action was taking place, terns swooped down behind the waves catching small fish, as gulls walked on the beach scavenging for any food they could find.

Another thing that attracted our attention was the shells. In those days, a plethora of shells littered the beach—there are much fewer today. Knobbed welks, channel welks, lightning whelks, olive shells, clams, scotch bonnets, moon snails, and auger shells, to name a few—all for the taking. When it was time to go home, we filled our pockets with these prizes. They became make-believe characters when we played in the sand in our grandparents' yard.

Between all these activities, I occasionally paused, captivated by the scene before us—grateful for the chance to be a part of such a natural miracle and to wonder at the events that had shaped this unique place and moment in time.

When Sister said it was time to go home, a great dread descended upon us—the walk home. The only thing we left behind on the beach were our footprints, which were soon erased by the wind and the next high tide. It was nearing midday, and the sun had time to heat the sand to an unbearable temperature for our bare feet. We hopped from one clump of vegetation to the next to avoid the blistering heat of the sand. It seemed an eternity before we reached the path that led to our grandparents' home. Next time, we promised ourselves, we would wear shoes to the beach . . .

CHAPTER 9

Going to Bed

From the sunny, gentle, wave-caressed beaches to the gray, wild, storm-ravaged shore, Hatteras is an island of contrasts. This characteristic makes it so appealing. For many, her brilliant days inspire an adventurous, independent spirit, while for some her nights spark apprehension. Aunt Katie was a victim of apprehension. After her husband died, she never spent another night at home alone. Understanding her anxiety, Grandmom invited her sister Katie to come across the road from her house and spend the nights with her, Pop Pop, and Sister.

Once Aunt Katie finished eating dinner and washing her dishes, she would check her house for any signs of fire in the kitchen, grab her white cotton nightgown, and cross the road to spend the night with us. The following day, before breakfast, she always went back home.

Every night at our house, after everyone had gone to bed, Aunt Katie would conduct one of her nightly fire inspections. To say she was compulsive would be an understatement. Her greatest fear was that a fire would consume the house where she was staying. Without fail, each night when everyone had settled in for a peaceful night's rest, Aunt Katie would get up and begin her search, starting with the downstairs rooms. After that part of the house passed her scrutiny, she would continue her investigation upstairs. It made no difference to her who was sleeping in a room; Aunt Katie would enter without hesitation, look under the bed, and sometimes even check under the covers of the sleeping occupants. How she navigated the darkened house without tripping and injuring herself will forever baffle me. Both my

Bedroom in my grandparents' house, with a slop bucket

brother and I were frightened more than once when we were suddenly awakened from a deep sleep by her searching for fire.

Her appearance was unsettling. She always wore a flowing, floor-length white cotton nightgown trailed behind her slender, bony figure as she walked. Her ashen face, wrinkled from over seventy years of exposure to the Hatteras sun, was framed by fine, straight white hair that fell to her neck. On bright, moonlit nights, when a soft glow dimly lit the house's rooms, she looked just like the apparition my brother and I imagined from one of the ghost tales Pop Pop told us. When Aunt Katie leaned over the bed and lifted the covers in search of fire, her presence could startle even the bravest. One night, she terrified Clifford so much that he spent the rest of the night sleeping with Sister.

Pop Pop, Grandmom, and Sister handled her nightly routine well. They never showed any signs of fear. My brother and I were horrified. We never knew whether what we were seeing was a ghost or Aunt Katie. We found it was best not to sleep until she finished her watch. After her first round of checks, she returned to bed, only to repeat her performance fifteen or twenty minutes later. Generally, after two inspections, she was satisfied that there was no fire danger and would drift off to sleep.

On one particular night, the mosquitoes were unusually thick. Instead of sitting on the pizer until dark to enjoy the evening breeze, as was our custom after supper, everyone, including my brother and me, settled in the sitting room to escape the bloodthirsty pests.

The conversation started by focusing on the day's events. Sister, who worked at the local grocery store, shared the news she had learned that day while at work. It seemed there was always someone who was either sick, had an accident, or had passed away. Pop Pop talked about his day at the fish house, telling us about the day's catch and how many boxes of fish he had iced. Grandmom told Aunt Katie about what she had prepared for dinner, and Aunt Katie did likewise. Grandmom served bacon, eggs, hot yeast rolls, apple butter or fruit jelly, molasses, and coffee for supper every night. So, that meal was never up for discussion. My brother and I called that menu "Hatteras supper." On occasion, we still enjoy it as an evening meal today.

Clifford, who was named after Pop Pop, and I were always captivated by the stories he shared, and he had an endless supply of fascinating tales in his repertoire. That night, he told us about walking home on a dark evening and seeing a white apparition fly from the road, disappearing into the adjacent marsh. Both my brother and I were eager and anxious to hear this story, but we always wished afterward that we hadn't. Aunt Katie was not amused; she was scared of her shadow. Grandmom was afraid of storms, but besides that, my grandparents and Sister were not frightened by anything.

My brother once asked Pop Pop, "What do you fear the most?" His reply was, "I'm not scared of anything." My brother said, "Well, I am." Pop Pop replied, "Then you're not living right." This profound statement lives with us both today.

A lull in conversation followed his story. Sister broke the silence as she grabbed the fly swatter hanging on a nail in the sitting room wall near the entrance to the kitchen, launching an assault on every mosquito she could find in the room. They usually landed near the upper wall by the ceiling, and if Sister spotted them, that's where they met their end. Each of us pointed out one or two pests for her to target. Dried, squashed, bloodstained mosquito bodies from past attacks stained the celadon-colored walls.

As darkness fell, there was a knock at the front door. It was Millard. He stood at the door, brushing mosquitoes off his clothes with a small branch covered in leaves from a myrtle bush. He used this tool to fend off the mosquitoes as he walked from his house along the sandy road to ours. He carefully brushed the mosquitoes off the screen door before letting himself inside. We recognized Millard as soon as he stepped onto the pizer. Millard was a deaf-mute whose only means of verbal communication were guttural sounds and laughter. As he stepped onto the pizer, he made distinctive grunting sounds while knocking the sand from his shoes by lightly stomping on the floor. Everyone on Hatteras recognized the sounds unique to this beloved island native. I always looked forward to his visits.

Grandmom and Aunt Katie had a sister who was deaf and mute and who died when she was thirteen years old. Grandmom learned to sign so she could communicate with her. However, her self-taught form of signing was limited since she only knew how to represent the letters of the alphabet on her hands. Since Grandmom was one of the few people in the village who knew how to sign, Millard frequently visited our family to have someone to "talk" to.

I was fascinated by the exchange between Millard and Grandmom. It was a show that captured everyone's attention. Millard signed to Grandmom, and she translated for everyone else in the room. We relayed any comments we had to Millard through her. Trying to understand the words they shared was a challenge. Even though Grandmom had taught me how to form the letters of the alphabet with my hands, I often struggled to interpret the words spelled by their rapidly moving fingers. Sister communicated with him by writing on Grandmom's tablet she kept in one of the sideboard's drawers. She passed Millard the tablet with her one-sentence statement or question. He replied with either a gesture or a one- or two-word note. Millard always had some village news that none of us had heard. He stayed about an hour, during which time Grandmom served everyone a piece of penny candy that she kept for special occasions in the upper right-hand drawer of the old sideboard in the sitting room.

Aunt Katie and her husband Monroe

After Millard left, Grandmom began her nightly routine before heading to bed. She said, "Young'uns, I think I'll turn in now." She then turned to Pop Pop and asked, "Clifford, did you bring the buckets in?" He didn't reply but got up from his wooden rocking chair and brought the buckets inside from the back porch.

We had no indoor plumbing. There was an outdoor toilet behind the house, but it was inconvenient to use at night. It was also scary to go to the outdoor toilet after dark. It took all the courage my brother and I could muster to use it during the day. Spiders and insects lurked in all sorts of hiding places. But the most alarming sight was the maggots living in the pit below the seats. The buckets in the house at night offered a welcome relief. Aunt

Katie, who slept downstairs, had a bucket in her bedroom, while Pop Pop placed the other one in the hallway upstairs. The rest of the family, who slept in the two bedrooms upstairs, shared it. Grandmom and Pop Pop had a bedroom on the southwest side of the house. My aunt, brother, and I slept in the northeast bedroom directly above Aunt Katie's room. Clifford and I shared a bed on one side of the small room, while my aunt's was on the other.

Grandmom went to the kitchen and filled a glass with water from the water bucket on a corner table by the back door. She then filled a second glass with water and placed her false teeth in it. She carried both glasses into the sitting room and set them on the sideboard.

Sitting in front of the sideboard mirror was an Aunt Jemimah cookie jar where she kept her medicine. Her entire apothecary consisted of a bottle of camphor, a bottle of mercurochrome, a vial of Carter's Little Liver Pills, a jar of Mentholatum salve, Ex-Lax, and a roll of Tums. She took out the jar of Mentholatum, unscrewed the cap, and dipped her little finger into the Vaseline-like contents. She then rubbed a thin layer of the menthol-laced salve in both her nostrils, stating that it "opened up her head" and helped her breathe better. After putting the Mentholatum back in place, she picked up the two glasses of water, one of which held her teeth, wished everyone a good night, and climbed the stairs to her bedroom.

Sister launched another fly swatter assault on the mosquitoes that managed to slip past Millard when he opened the screen door on his way out. After returning her weapon to the nail by the kitchen door, she reached under a table in the corner of the room by Grandmom's wooden rocking chair and pulled out a spray gun. It consisted of a glass jar filled with an insect-killing liquid. The threaded mouth of the jar allowed someone to screw it onto a metal handle containing a piston-like plunger, which forced air through an atomizer at the end of the handle above the jar. The device released a fine mist when someone pressed the plunger inward. She soaked each of the screens in the house with the insecticide. The odor lingered for most of the night.

Aunt Katie and Sister were the next to retire. Pop Pop joked with my brother and me before we followed the others to bed. When we heard the ringing sound caused by a liquid hitting the bottom of the white porcelain bucket upstairs, we knew Grandmom was not long before getting into bed.

This night, I deliberately waited until everyone else left the sitting room. Once the coast was clear, I opened the Aunt Jemima cookie jar, took out the jar of Mentholatum, and slipped it into my pocket. I moved to the center of the sitting room, stood on my tiptoes, and reached for the string that hung from the on/off switch of the ceramic light fixture on the ceiling. I pulled the string, cutting off the power to the bare sixty-watt bulb. Light from another bare bulb in a similar fixture in the upstairs hallway illuminated the steps well enough for me to see to make my way up to my bedroom.

After my brother and I put on our pajamas, he was next to "use the bucket" that sat outside our doorway. The ring was sharper and louder when the family's males used the bucket. It lacked the hissing sound that accompanied the ring made by the females. When he returned to get in bed, it was my turn at the pot. After I finished, I placed a lid over the top to help control the odor of what was now a bucket one-fourth full of waste.

It was a ritual for me to jump between Pop Pop and Grandmom in their bedroom and land into the fluffy feather bed, which was plump in the middle because the feathers and air had shifted from each side of the bed where they lay. The sheets were damp from the ever-present summer humidity.

A light, sweet, sour, musty odor from our unwashed bodies filled my nostrils. It was not an offensive scent but one that set us apart from others, one that indicated similar chemistry, one that suggested we were family. Since our only source of freshwater came from rain, we had to conserve water. A weekly Saturday bath was the custom.

Nowhere have I ever felt safer than when I was snuggling between my grandmother and granddaddy, engulfed in that feather bed. Pop Pop and I giggled and laughed while Grandmom pretended to be asleep. A hissing sound from the bucket signaled that Sister was about to settle into her bed. When I heard her putting the lid back on, I carefully climbed out of my grandparents' bed, making sure not to knock over the glass of water that held Grandmom's false teeth and her drinking water, which she had sitting together on the floor beside the bed. I don't know how she could tell the difference between the two in the dark when she woke up thirsty at night. I quickly crossed the pitch-black hall, entered my room, and climbed into bed with my brother.

My brother and I remained awake until Aunt Katie finished her final search for fire in our room. Shortly after, we heard a muffled ring from the slop bucket downstairs, which signaled that she was about to retire for the night. We waited about fifteen minutes to make sure that she was asleep. Sister was snoring in the bed across the room from us.

I whispered to my brother, "Did you find some twine?"

"Yes," he replied in a hushed voice as he retrieved it from under his pillow and passed it to me. "Grandmom had some in one of the drawers of her sewing machine."

"How long is it?" I said.

"Long enough," he said.

I reached under my pillow, where I had hidden the Mentholatum jar. I unscrewed the top, placed one end of the string into the jar, and replaced the lid. The jar was securely attached to the end of the string.

We sneaked to the window and peered into the dark obscurity. It was a typical Hatteras night before the convenience of streetlights. The only light source outside the homes came from the stars or the bioluminescence of some of nature's local creatures. All we could see was a spectacular light show created by fireflies dancing over the marsh in the moonless void beyond the cheesecloth screen that covered the opening of our raised bedroom window. The darkness made it impossible to see your hand in front of your face—a night whose mysterious sounds could easily inspire legendary tales of unexplained phenomena. Tales that could make your hair stand on end.

We pushed out one end of the insecticide-soaked screen and lowered the Mentholatum jar below the downstairs window. When the jar swung like the pendulum of Grandmom's chiming clock, we directed it to rake and knock against the side of the house. Then we stopped and listened. There was nothing but silence. After a second round of knocks and rakes outside Aunt Katie's window, we finally received the response we had hoped for.

With terror in her voice, Aunt Katie yelled, "Merciful Father, what on earth is making that racket?"

We heard her bolt across the dark bedroom, kicking the slop bucket as she reached the doorway into the sitting room, where just a few hours before, Pop Pop told us the story of seeing an apparition. We quickly retrieved the Mentholatum jar and jumped into bed, pretending to be asleep.

In no time, Aunt Katie stood at the top of the stairs in the small hallway, wringing her hands and breathlessly shouting, "Mag, Clifford, wake up! There's something outside my bedroom window."

By this time, everyone was awake. Grandmom and Pop Pop quickly emerged from their room as Sister hurriedly crossed our room toward the door. With convincing looks of innocence and concern on our faces, Clifford and I followed Sister. Aunt Katie was standing outside our bedroom door. Her floor-length nightgown, now drenched with the contents of the slop bucket she kicked over in her haste to wake up the family, clung to her legs. Panicked, she told us about the knocking and scraping sounds outside her bedroom window.

Grandmom, Pop Pop, and Sister followed her downstairs and into the pitch-black Hatteras night to investigate the situation. While everyone was outside, I rushed downstairs and returned the Mentholatum container to Aunt Jemimah. I dashed back up the stairs and into my room. Clifford and I laughed and joyfully danced, celebrating having paid Aunt Katie back for all the times she had frightened us. When we heard the adults return after finding no signs of what had caused Aunt Katie's distress, we quickly jumped into bed and spent the rest of the night dreaming of sweet revenge.

CHAPTER 10

Going to the Picture Show

In addition to walking to the landing on Friday night, Saturday was the only other evening of the week that Grandmom would allow me to leave the house after supper. I could go to a movie at Mr. Ander's movie theater on the village's main road in the heart of Hatteras. I received clear instructions to come home right after the picture show ended.

Aside from church, the weekly picture show was the only time when a crowd of fifty or more gathered in the community. Since television didn't reach the Outer Banks until the late 1950s, going to the movies was a special occasion. Unlike the solemn Sunday morning church gatherings, Saturday nights at the picture show had a lively, festive atmosphere.

I eagerly looked forward to my Saturday night ritual—taking a bath, wearing a clean shirt and shorts, eating supper, and heading out barefoot for an evening of fun with my friends. It was also at these movie nights that I, like many others, began to take notice of the opposite sex.

However, one thing always dampened the excitement of the night—something I dreaded every Saturday. The walk back to my grandparents' house, usually around 9:30 p.m., was unsettling even when I had company. But walking home alone? That was downright terrifying, especially on one particular night.

As always, I began preparing for the big Saturday night event early in the afternoon, around 3:00 p.m. Without indoor plumbing, bathing was quite an ordeal.

The movie theater, circa 1950s

First, I heated a kettle of water on the gas stove, then gathered a towel and washcloth from the old washstand and searched the kitchen for a soap bar. After that, I filled a small porcelain-enameled basin with cold water from the cistern. Because there was no bathroom, I had to carry everything up the steep steps to my bedroom—a tricky balancing act that made getting clean even more challenging.

Everyone in the family took a bath in the privacy of their bedrooms. Since our only source of fresh water was rainwater collected from rain on our roof, which we needed to conserve, everyone limited their weekly Saturday bath to the equivalent of a couple of kettles of water.

Some weeks, after a heavy rain, Grandmom would let me bathe on the back porch in her #2 zinc washtub. Rainwater flowed through gutters and downspouts from the roof into a cistern beside the house. If it rained sometime around Saturday and we remembered, my grandfather would redirect one of the downspouts into the washtub. The tub, which Grandmom usually used for rinsing her clothes, was filled about two-thirds full before Pop Pop returned the downspout to the cistern. After the rain shower passed and the clouds cleared, the sun's rays warmed the water to a comfortable temperature for bathing. A tub bath was a rare treat only enjoyed by my brother and me. The adults in the family never bathed outside on the back porch, even though the cover of a large fig tree would have hidden them from view during this Saturday ritual. Besides, they were too big to fit in the tub anyway.

I don't remember the location of my bath on this particular Saturday, but I was squeaky clean and dressed by suppertime for my night out on the town. After, which always featured the same favorites—eggs, bacon, apple butter or jam, molasses, hot yeast rolls, and coffee—I was given a quarter for my movie ticket and ten cents for candy and a Pepsi. I left home for the picture show around 6:00, even though the film started an hour later.

As I reached the end of the path connecting our yard to the road, I met Mac, who had also taken his Saturday bath and dressed for the evening's event. A year younger than me, Mac was a neighborhood friend who lived a few houses to the north.

We exchanged greetings and eagerly set off toward the movie theater. Neither of us knew what film was playing, and neither of us cared. The movies were usually black and white and at least five years old, but that didn't matter. The real excitement was getting out of the house and enjoying a night of freedom.

I noticed that Mac was carrying two pieces of rope, each about six feet long.

"What you doin' with that rope?" I asked.

"Goin' to have some fun," he replied with a twinkle in his eye.

"What kinda fun?" I wanted to know.

"Oh, you'll see," he replied in his Hatteras dialect, which some have described as sounding like an English Cockney.

I thought, "What kind of fun can you have with two pieces of dry-rot rope that were not even fit to tie a skiff to a dock?"

An hour before the movie began, every child in Hatteras Village older than eight had gathered at Mr. Ander's store next to the movie theater. About forty-five minutes later, the adults attending the show started to arrive.

Mr. Ander's store featured a spacious, covered front porch filled with kids. Some sat at the edge of the porch, dangling their legs and tracing patterns in the sand with their toes. Others gathered in groups, interacting just like any group of adolescents might. Laughter erupted from one group and then another. The atmosphere of controlled merriment intensified as the crowd grew larger. Two steps above the porch was the entrance of the old general store, which had been in business since 1916. From the open office area, Mr. Ander, the proprietor—a small, stooped-over, rather frail man—sternly observed the cheerful native kids coming in to purchase their refreshments for the movie.

Two items set this store apart from others in the village. One was a large wooden fifty-gallon barrel full of delicious dark molasses which was pumped into jars supplied by the store's patrons. A frothy, sea foam layer floated on the freshly filled containers. However, the most popular attraction in the store was an endless display case of penny candy. Since only popcorn was available in the movie theater's foyer and drinks were not offered, a ten-cent bag of penny candy from the store became the favorite treat during adventures to faraway places on the small silver screen.

Choosing which candy to buy was always a delightful struggle—like picking just one star from a sky full of twinkling lights. Everything in the glass-enclosed showcase beckoned me with its bright colors and sugary scents, making my decision even harder. But despite my best efforts to branch out, I almost always ended up with the same selection: four two-inch squares of fiery red cinnamon hard candy, a four-inch stick of red-and-white-striped peppermint, a matching piece of red-and-green striped wintergreen, two BB Bats, a Mary Jane, and one soft white square of coconut candy. Occasionally, I'd trade a few pieces for a soft drink.

As I was paying for my candy, the sound of skidding tires sliced through the hum of the crowd, followed by a burst of laughter. Mr. Ander's wife, Miss Inez, who was working that night, passed me a small brown bag filled with my candy. Gripping it tightly, I hurried outside, eager to see what had caused the commotion.

Even on a Saturday night, traffic on the road in front of the store was sparse. Sometimes, fifteen minutes or more passed without a single car passing by.

A flustered, visibly irritated driver was speeding away as I stepped outside. It didn't take long to figure out what had happened—Mac and five other boys had been up to their usual mischief, and this time, their unfortunate target was Mr. Garland. Home on leave from his job on a dredge in Florida, he was a serious, no-nonsense bachelor—hardly the type to laugh off a prank.

A glance at the scene in front of the store made it clear that Mac's idea of "havin' some fun" involved ropes—though exactly how I was about to find out.

The boys had carefully crafted their prank like a fisherman setting a clever trap. They spread a thin, two-inch-wide strip of golden Hatteras sand across the freshly paved black asphalt, creating a striking contrast. At each end of the sand line, Mac's two ropes extended beyond the road's edge, their loose ends held by three boys on either side.

To an approaching driver, it looked like a single rope stretched taut across the road. The boys positioned themselves as if they were ready to pull, giving the illusion that the "rope" would suddenly be lifted several feet into the air just as a vehicle approached.

As Mr. Garland's brand-new 1952 Mercury neared, the boys yanked back on their ropes, making it seem like an obstacle was about to rise in his path. Like any cautious driver, he reacted instinctively—slamming the brakes to avoid what appeared to be a dangerous obstruction. The tires screeched against the pavement, sending up the sound of protest, while the boys laughed at their trick's success.

The sound echoed across the village, followed by a wave of laughter from the onlookers. The practical jokers tumbled backward in the sand, laughing and rolling at the hilarious scene. Mr. Garland sat in his car, seething. A few expletives slipped from the light blue Mercury as he sped away from the scene, provoking another round of laughter from the spectators. For the next fifteen minutes, everyone recounted the scene repeatedly. The volume of laughter rose up each time a group of kids retold the story of the prank.

Just before the movie started, Roberta arrived at the theater to sell tickets. To me, her beauty was as radiant as the morning sun over the ocean. Her deeply tanned, smooth skin contrasted elegantly with her sundress, its delicate cord shoulder straps resting on her sun-kissed shoulders. Her brown eyes, framed by dark brows and long lashes, shimmered warmly, while her shoulder-length brunette hair cascaded effortlessly around her face. (Yes, I was indeed noticing the opposite sex.)

The whites of her eyes and the bold red of her lipstick perfectly complemented the crisp white fabric of her dress, patterned with scarlet hibiscus flowers. No Hollywood actress could rival her beauty. There were many pretty girls on Hatteras, but to me, Roberta was in a league of her own—the unattainable dream of every young man. Standing at the ticket booth, handing over my admission, and stealing a few moments to admire her was worth the price of the movie.

Roberta flashed a smile from behind the glass partition as she took my quarter and slid my ticket through the half-circle opening—an invisible boundary between me and a beauty who would never see me as more than just another kid at the Saturday night movie. No matter what film awaited inside, I had already received more than my money's worth. That brief exchange, that fleeting smile, was enough even before I stepped through the door, and the projector began to roll.

Inside the white, rectangular clapboard theater, built in 1932 and topped with a green-and-red zigzag-striped shingled roof, the seats were arranged in two sections, separated by a central aisle. The young patrons filled the seats near the front, while the adults opted for those in the back. As everyone settled in, music from a 45-rpm record player filled the room with a popular tune, creating a flat, dimensionless sound.

Most boys and girls paired up when they entered the theater, contrasting with the same-sex groups gathered outside the theater on Mr. Ander's store porch. I sat beside Ruby, a neighborhood friend who lived near our house. We were just friends, nothing more—we were eleven years old. Earlier that week, we had jokingly suggested sitting together at the movies. I found myself following through on such a plan for the first time. I kept it to myself, knowing my folks at home would probably tease me if they found out I was planning to sit with a girl at the picture show.

Ruby bought her ticket and walked in ahead of me. An impatient patron shoved me away from the ticket booth as I stood captivated by Roberta's beauty. I resisted his push, savoring one last look. Only then did I step inside. I found Ruby and sat beside her. Did we even talk? I think not.

While waiting for the movie to begin, Ruby chatted with her friends while I joked around with mine. She enjoyed candy from her brown paper bag, and I savored candy from mine. It wasn't until the lights dimmed that we finally acknowledged each other's presence.

At 7 p.m., few sporadic stomps from a handful of impatient patrons started the commotion. Soon, the old wooden floor erupted in a thunderous roar as everyone joined in to let Shank, Mr. Ander's son who ran the projectors, know it was time to start the show. At ten minutes past seven, the movie still hadn't started. The floor endured several more brutal assaults from the mainly barefoot, impatient customers. Shank announced that the delay was due to a burned-out projection lamp. He had ordered one, which would arrive soon on the Midgett Bus Line—a public transportation link between Hatteras and the mainland.

The bus was supposed to arrive at 5:00 p.m., but a delay occurred when it got stuck on the beach between Oregon Inlet and Buxton. It was the only bus line in the country that traveled forty miles of its route along the beachfront, since there were no paved roads. As we all knew, getting stuck in the sand was common. When this happened to the bus, the driver asked all the passengers to disembark. Armed with shovels and sheer strength, they assisted Stocky, the driver and owner of this unique bus line, eventually freeing the vehicle from the sand—and often repeating the effort a few miles further down the beach. Today was one of those days, and the trip to Hatteras was extended by a half hour or so. And today, of all days, the bus was carrying an essential item that stood between Hatteras movie buffs and an adventure on the silver screen.

Shank assured us that the movie would start in five minutes. A cheer and another thunderous roar of bare feet stomping against the wooden floor resonated off the walls of the old theater. Eventually, the movie began.

At some point during the movie's first half, my right hand accidentally brushed against Ruby's left. That slight touch must have signaled something to her because, before I knew it, she clasped my hand tightly—like an old, hard crab latching onto its prey. I froze, stunned by what was happening, but didn't dare pull away. The longer she held on, the more I liked it.

Eventually, I stopped being a nervous bystander and became an eager hand-holder.

Ruby was cute, but she wasn't Roberta, and yet, in the dim glow of the theater, with my heart pounding in a way it never had before, she might as well have been. Each time the film broke—something that happened often—the lights flickered on, and we quickly let go, pretending nothing had happened. But as soon as the movie flickered back to life, so did we. Our hands stayed intertwined until The End appeared on the screen. When the theater lights came up for good, we hesitated before awkwardly slipping apart and heading toward the exit, our shared secret still warm between our palms.

Without saying goodbye to each other, she joined her friends, and I went to mine. We left the theater into the pitch-black, moonless night that awaited beyond its doors. We passed the empty ticket booth where Roberta had stolen my heart two hours earlier and sold me a ticket to a fantasy I still remember today.

While we were in the theater, the wind had picked up quite a bit from the southwest, and thunder rumbled over the ocean. A thunderstorm would soon draw near shore, but I was confident there was ample time to get home.

Mr. Ander's store was now dimly lit, and he had turned the porch lights off. Before I headed up the road to Grandmom's house, I must have spent more time than I realized standing in front of the store with friends, reminiscing about the incident with the rope. When I turned the corner at Mr. Dolph's grocery store on my way home, I noticed that everyone going my way had left me and I had to navigate the dark Hatteras night alone. With no streetlights, the darkness swallowed the village whole—a thick, inky void that hid even the stars.

As I passed the old weather bureau on my left, the large white wooden structure was barely visible in the darkness. I spotted Mr. Damon's house and his barbershop, the last landmarks near the road before reaching Cousin Willie's old home. The house had been abandoned for years and now served as a funeral home. Uncle Horton was the undertaker, proprietor, and jack of all trades. Despite his efforts with the place, time had taken its toll. It was a shadow of its former self, desperately in need of a fresh coat of paint. The green shutters, faded and crooked, dangled from the windows like broken wings. It was barely visible though it sat close to the road, framed by two ancient live oaks draped in Spanish moss, their limbs reaching out like gnarled hands. As I approached the eerie house, my pulse quickened. Still racing from handholding at the movie and the darkness of the night, my heart seemed to stutter. I was unsure if it could handle any more stress. This heartbeat differed from the one I felt while holding Ruby's hand. That had produced an exhilarating sensation. This was one of pure terror.

All I could think about as I approached the funeral home was the cold, lifeless body of a local resident inside. They had set the funeral for Sunday afternoon at the Methodist church. I kept to the right side of the sandy road, staying as far away from the house as possible. I didn't dare even glance in that direction. I was so close to the edge of the road that, occasionally, red cedar branches from the trees in front of Miss Ursa's house slapped me as the wind from the approaching storm stirred them into a frenzy. Miss Ursa lived directly across from the funeral home. Getting past that funeral home

Ursa and Nelson Stowe's home, which was right across from the funeral home

felt like an eternity. As I hurried by, I never saw the sheets Uncle Horton had washed and spread over some myrtle bushes to dry. Moments after I passed, a strong gust of wind caught one of the sheets, tumbling across the road in front of me like a ghostly apparition. My feet scarcely touched the ground until I landed on the pizer of Grandmom's house.

Everyone had gone to bed except for my Aunt Essie. Without swatting away the mosquitoes before entering the house, I dashed into the sitting room, where she awaited me.

"Honey, what in the world is wrong?" she asked me.

"Sister, the dead person in the funeral home just passed me on the road!" I could scarcely talk I was so out of breath.

"Now, Sugar, there ain't no dead person going to bother you," she said, but I was not easily convinced.

My story of terror wasn't the only one. Sunday morning before Sunday school, Mac told me how he had helped Uncle Horton carry a body into the funeral home on Friday morning. That night, in a manly effort to impress his girlfriend, Mac broke into the funeral home to show her the embalming room. With no lights to guide them, the two intruders went to the old kitchen at the back of the house, which was now the embalming room. As they crossed the floor, Mac suddenly felt something grab him around the neck. Whatever it was seemed to yank him back, throwing him off balance and crashing him to the floor. He let out a terrified yell that sent his girlfriend bolting from the back door and racing up the road without him.

When Mac looked up from the floor, he realized that his neck had become entangled in a loop of rubber hose attached to an apparatus hanging above him. A pole near the embalming table connected an embalming fluid container at one end and a large needle hanging on the other. At that moment, however, Mac, the rubber hose, the stainless-steel fluid container—still holding leftover embalming fluid from earlier that afternoon—and the needle were all scattered across the old kitchen floor. Mac quickly ran to the same door his "dearly departed" girlfriend had used. Before long, he was back home, feeling relieved to be there.

While walking home after Sunday school, I overheard Mac telling his friends an embellished version of his experience at the funeral home—about how he had broken into the funeral home, been tackled by a dead man, and witnessed the undertakers burying the deceased's blood in the backyard. Had I known any of this, my walk home after the movie that night would have been even more frightening.

The following Monday, while I was climbing in the live oaks in front of our house, Ruby walked down our path and into the yard.

"Hoi," she said in her Hatteras brogue. "Whatcha doing?"

"Climbing," I said. "What you doing down here?"

Ruby lived up the road from us. Since "up" and "down" were relative terms used by the villagers to describe locations along the route, I lived down from her.

"I brought you something," she said with a big smile.

She reached into her shorts pocket and pulled out a narrow silver ring.

"My uncle made it for me from a nickel. I want you to have it."

"Thanks," I said as I slipped the ring on my finger. It was a perfect fit.

"You want a climb some?" I said.

"I 'magine," she said.

She jumped and grabbed a branch just above her head. Flipping backward and upside down, she extended her feet and legs over a limb. Swinging first by her legs, she pulled herself up and sat on the branch. There was a sparkle in her eye, and I'm sure I had a twinkle in mine, too.

The following Saturday, Mama and Daddy arrived at Hatteras from Washington to carry my brother and me back home. Our summer stay at Hatteras was over for another year; it was time to head back to school. I never went to the movies with Ruby again.

Somehow, that following summer, things felt different. I lost the keepsake she had given me during the winter, but I never told her. The ring is gone, but the memories of that night remain vivid to this day.

CHAPTER 11

Going to the Post Office

Back when the world beyond Hatteras seemed as distant as the mainland beyond our watery horizon—a time with no television, no telephone, and certainly no internet—the post office was the island's lifeline. That's where the world reached us, tucked inside envelopes and brown paper packages. It was our small gateway to the world, bringing letters from Mama and, now and then, that cherished Sears and Roebuck catalog, whose pages we thumbed through as if it were a wish book from heaven. Knowing all this, you can imagine the thrill I felt making my daily walk to the post office— sand crunching underfoot, heart pounding with excitement—wondering what treasures might be waiting inside for me and the family.

Established in 1858, the post office in Hatteras Village was the first on Hatteras Island. At the island's southern tip, the village grew in importance during that period. The opening of Hatteras Inlet in 1846 created a deep-water channel, attracting more boats and trade. As maritime activity increased, it was only natural for the postal service to establish itself in Hatteras Village before any other island settlement. People described the building as "tiny as an outhouse, with ragged boards and crooked steps." You'd have to turn sideways to get out, and there weren't even separate mailboxes.

Jumping ahead to the 1930s and 1940s, mail reached Hatteras by small boats that delivered just one and rarely two bags of mail. If foul weather struck and Pamlico Sound was rougher than Grandmom's old washboard, delivery stopped completely. Later, after a ferry began running at Oregon Inlet, trucks bounced and bumped their way down the beach to Hatteras. In

The old post office

the 1940s and early 1950s, a daily bus route ran from Hatteras to Manteo, carrying both passengers and mail. Yet even with wheels replacing boats, storms and ocean overwash could still halt the mail run, as if Mother Nature herself were the postmistress of the US mail to be delivered.

When I spent summers with my grandparents, the post office had moved into a larger, yet weathered building—modest and slightly leaning from storms, but still the dependable center of village life. A few creaking wooden steps led to a covered porch where villagers gathered each morning, waiting for the mail to be delivered.

Inside the small, one-room building, a partition separated the space into two sections: one for the public and one for the postmaster's work. The public side was lined with orderly rows of shiny metal mailboxes, each faintly gleaming in the light. Behind that wall, the postmaster's office buzzed with activity as mail was sorted and placed for delivery. There were two dials on the metal mailbox door. With their correct combination, opening our boxes felt like unlocking a secret door to the outside world. The air inside carried a faint scent of paper and wood polish, while neighbors exchanged quiet greetings and the soft jingle of box doors marked the morning routine.

Home delivery has never existed in Hatteras—and that's still true today. If you want to receive your mail, you must go to the post office and collect it from your assigned box.

One of my favorite stories about postal delivery in Hatteras came from my mother. Born in 1916, she knew a Hatteras that now exists only in memory. In her childhood, the mail arrived by mailboat, a lifeline from the wider world.

Next to her house was a pond about half the size of a football field—large enough to paddle a small skiff, its surface smooth as a mirror under a windless, sunny sky. Two other homes sat along the water's edge as well: Mr. Curtis's and Cousin Willie's.

At the time, there was no indoor plumbing, so each house had its own outdoor toilet. But these weren't ordinary outhouses. They sat on wooden pilings about a yard above the pond and were connected to each property by short piers. The pond was flushed twice daily by the tide through a narrow ditch leading to the sound.

A child's imagination can turn even the simplest things into an adventure. Mama and a friend would play "mailboat" on that pond. They tore pages from an old Sears catalog and folded them into envelope-sized parcels, pretending they were mail. A flat-bottomed dinghy, just big enough for two kids, was tied to her family's pier. For hours, she and a friend paddled from toilet to toilet, delivering their pretend mail. In their minds, they transformed a quiet pond into a lively Pamlico Sound, delivering mail to a series of island village post offices of their own creation.

I can still picture myself walking beside Pop Pop down the sandy road to the post office about half a mile from our house, right in the heart of the village. The sun was usually warm on our backs. The dull crunch of sand underfoot set the pace for our little adventure. The sandy, deep road made the walk tiring, but the chance of a letter or a Sears catalog made every step worth it. Back then, only important notices, bills, and Mama's letters arrived—no junk mail. Postage for a letter was three cents, marked by a blue stamp with Thomas Jefferson's profile. Postcards cost a penny and were light tan, printed

Toilets over the pond

with a green one-cent stamp showing George Washington's image in an oval frame, "U.S. POSTAGE" above and "ONE CENT" below.

Mr. Job, the postmaster, lived with his wife and daughters in the house just behind the post office. He was a man of average height, always neatly dressed in a white shirt and tie, with a pipe clenched between his teeth like a captain steady at the helm. He greeted everyone with the easy politeness of a man who knew his place at the heart of village life. His face stood out among the men of Hatteras—smooth, not weathered at all, as if his work behind the mail counter had spared him from the salt and sun that had carved the others' faces like driftwood left too long on the shore.

"Morning to you, Mr. Clifford," Mr. Job said, his voice calm and sure, carrying the warmth of good manners. "How're you and Buddy faring on this warm day?"

"Why, me and the boy are doing just fine," Pop Pop said, his eyes crinkling. "Just stopped in to see if the mail truck brought us anything today."

"I think I just put something in your box just a few minutes ago," replied Mr. Job.

Pop Pop walked me over to the bank of metal mailboxes. He leaned down and quietly said, "I'm going to teach you how to open our box. So pay attention to what I show you."

Pop Pop after a storm, with the post office to the left

"See these here dials?" he said, pointing at the mailbox.

"Yes, sir," I replied.

"Well, this one on this here left side needs to be turn't to one notch before the letter D," he said as he turned the knob on the left-hand side of the box.

"And this here other knob needs to be turn't two notches past the letter T." This time adjusting the knob on the right-hand side of the box.

"In other words . . . It's a quarter to D and a half past T. Do you got it?"

"Yes, sir!" I said with the enthusiasm of someone who had just won the lottery.

"Now the box will open by sliding over this here small lever under the left-hand knob," he said proudly. "Now you try it."

I reached up and slid the lever over, and the box popped right open.

Pop Pop immediately closed the mailbox door, twisted both knobs several times, and said, "Now you try it."

In my mind, I repeated the rhythmic phrase that could open my world at

Hatteras to somewhere beyond: "A quarter to D and a half past T. A quarter to D and a half past T."

I adjusted the knobs to the correct combination and then slid the small lever beneath the left-hand dial; the box clicked open. A grin spread across my face—pure triumph.

I looked up at my granddaddy and said, with all the confidence I could muster, "Now I can go down the road and get the mail for you anytime you want me to."

A white envelope caught my eye, propped at a slight angle inside the small mailbox. I reached in and pulled it out—my name and my brother's name were on it, written in Mama's familiar hand. She wrote my brother and me about twice a week while we spent the summers with our aunt and grandparents. Each letter felt like a treasure. My heart gave a little leap—I couldn't wait to open it.

I decided to wait until I got home, but the trip back seemed to take forever. The moment I reached the house, I burst through the door calling for my little brother, "Clifford! We got a letter from Mama!"

He hurried over, and we both rushed outside to our favorite old oak tree for climbing. We scrambled onto our usual branch and sat side by side. My hands trembled as I tore open the envelope. As I read, I could almost hear Mama's voice—her news from home spilling off the page. And then came the best part: she was coming to visit us next week!

CHAPTER 12

Going on Vacation

Each year, our daily routine shifted when Mama and Daddy arrived for their midsummer vacation in Hatteras. Sometimes, this was a welcome change, while at other times, it was not.

Mama was born and raised in Hatteras. She was the youngest of two daughters. At nineteen, she left home to attend Tayloe Hospital School of Nursing in Washington, a small, sleepy coastal town in North Carolina on the then-pristine Pamlico River. The morning she departed Hatteras on the freight boat for nursing training—which in those days meant not only an education but also three years of indentured servitude at the hospital, her father said, "Naomi, honey, I'll see you back here in a week." He was sure his daughter would become homesick and want to return to Hatteras. She did get homesick, sometimes crying for hours, but she never returned except for weekend visits and vacations.

Daddy met Mama when she was a student nurse. He took quite a liking to her—so much that he wanted to keep her around permanently after she graduated. They got married, and a few years later—just shy of a year before the Japanese bombed Pearl Harbor—I made my grand entrance into the world. My brother Clifford was born in 1946, just a year after Hiroshima. While in school, he was assigned to write his biography, and in true younger-sibling fashion, he summed up his grand arrival with this gem: "They dropped the atomic bomb in 1945, and one year later, my mother dropped me." Timing is everything.

Swain family, 1950s

Mama was a nurse who practiced her profession with an unforgettable smile and immense compassion. In addition, she gained her nursing knowledge not only from years of training and study but also from extensive on-the-job experience. Everyone who knew her could see that she was one of those rare individuals who was an exceptional credit to her profession. When she committed herself to something, she gave it her undivided dedication, whether it was her work, children, or marriage.

Hatteras was more than just a vacation spot for my mother—it was her harbor where she could drop anchor and find peace. She wasn't just taking a break from the mainland but returning to where she grew up—her home.

Even though getting to Hatteras was an arduous journey, each visit was a reunion with the tide of love and security she had known since childhood. Spending time there with her parents wasn't just a getaway; it was a chance to refill the well of the connection she so profoundly missed.

Daddy's parents raised him and his ten brothers and sisters on a tenant farm on the mainland in Beaufort County. Daddy's formal education ended in the tenth grade. According to him, his twin sister Lillian told their father everything he did wrong at school. He grew weary of her constant evaluations, so he dropped out. He worked several jobs without a formal education until he found his niche as a salesman. In this role, he earned a living selling mattresses and box springs in rural communities from the back of a pickup truck. He was as exceptional a salesman as my mother was a nurse. He could sell sand in the Sahara as effortlessly as my mother could heal with a touch.

His dark side, however, was alcoholism—a storm that didn't break until after my brother and I were born. As much as I hated the tempests of his drunken binges, they were the winds that carried me to Hatteras each summer. During those months, my mother anchored my brother and me in the safe harbor of her parents and sister, knowing their steady presence would shelter us from the unpredictable tides at home.

Since Daddy was self-employed and had the luxury of taking time off whenever he chose, he always vacationed in Hatteras when Mama took a break from work. However, he was one of those individuals who wasn't particularly fond of Hatteras; it had very little to offer him. Daddy didn't like walking on the beach, swimming, crabbing, clamming, or doing any other pleasurable activity the island provided. He enjoyed fishing when the fish were biting; otherwise, he was bored. Daddy didn't like reading, so curling up with a captivating book wasn't an option. I'm confident he has never read a book in his life. Besides reading the daily newspaper, I only recall seeing him read for pleasure once: it was an article in Redbook magazine. When he finished it, you'd have thought he had read the entire series of *The Story of Civilization* by Will and Ariel Durant.

Daddy didn't want to endure anything he didn't enjoy, so why did he vacation at Hatteras? Simple—he was putting on a show. He had a knack for making himself seem more successful than he indeed was, a skill that served him well as a salesman. Taking an annual vacation—especially when many of his peers couldn't afford such a luxury—was his way of crafting an image of success, a postcard-perfect illusion for his friends back home. The reality was that this vacation did not cost him any more than if he had stayed home.

To keep himself busy—and maybe justify the trip—he'd haul a truckload of mattresses to sell. At the same time, the rest of us soaked up everything Hatteras had to offer. Aside from indulging in Grandmom and Mama's mouthwatering seafood, the island never suited him.

He was a talented musician, and every night after supper, when the local folks dropped by, he'd settle in with his banjo and play for hours. His repertoire included everything from "Boil Them Cabbage Down" to "The Old Rugged Cross," but to my ears, it all blended into one relentless racket. The sharp twang of the strings and the hollow reverberation of the banjo head bouncing off the walls of our small sitting room felt less like music and more like an assault on my eardrums. A single night of this high-pitched picking and strumming was tolerable. Still, night after night, it became a test of endurance. Still, everyone else seemed to love it, and he relished every moment in the spotlight.

When my parents arrived, it was a bittersweet moment for me. As Daddy's truck—loaded with mattresses—reached the end of the path leading into my grandparents' front yard, I was overjoyed to see Mama, whom I hadn't seen in three or four weeks. However, Daddy's presence often brought an air of anxiety. It was much like the anxiety I used to feel while watching the tall, multilayered cumulonimbus clouds hovering over the ocean, with their sharp lightning and loud claps of thunder bursting into a violent summer storm that threatened the idyllic Hatteras setting. None of us ever knew if his vacation would turn into hell. It had happened so many times before.

One year, I stood on the pizer until the truck stopped in front of the house, then ran to the passenger side to open the door and give Mama a big hug and kiss. It was a long embrace filled with unspoken words: I love you, I've missed you, and I'm happy we're together again. Her broad grin showed her joy at being in Hatteras with her family and boys. She couldn't hug my brother and me enough.

For this visit, she wore a brand-new summer outfit: a pair of peach-colored knee-length shorts and a matching white cotton top she had purchased at Charles Store, a discount franchise in Washington. Stylish white sandals with thin straps complemented the bright red coat of nail polish on her toenails.

Daddy was next in line for a hug, and the first thing I always noticed was the scent of Vitalis, the slick touch of his carefully combed hair contrasting with Mama's soft warmth. His hugs were never quite like hers—polite, fleeting, more of a gesture than an embrace. I suspect his reserved nature came from growing up in a household of eleven siblings, where affection was a luxury his parents simply didn't have time to teach him. Though he and his family were kind, there was a certain self-focus about them, a contrast to the openhearted warmth of my mother and her parents. Perhaps that's the key to a genuinely affectionate hug—the ability to give without holding back.

Daddy dressed for a Hatteras summer as if he were heading to a board meeting. While Mother embraced the island's laid-back vibe with casual attire, he stuck to his signature look—long black pants, a crisp white short-sleeve dress shirt, black socks, polished black shoes, and a brimmed hat straight out of a 1930s gangster film. He may have been on vacation, but his wardrobe never got the memo.

After my brother and I hugged our parents, Grandmom, Pop Pop, and Sister turned their attention to my parents with their usual warm welcome.

Pop Pop helped Daddy carry the luggage into my parents' bedroom, the largest of the two downstairs. The luggage mainly consisted of brown paper bags, a couple of sturdy cardboard boxes, and a two-tone tan suitcase Mama had purchased many years ago from the Woolworth store in Washington.

When our parents visited, my brother Clifford, too afraid to sleep alone downstairs, always stayed in the bedroom next to theirs. This arrangement meant I also got to sleep alone since Clifford and I shared one of the two beds in Sister's room upstairs when our parents weren't visiting.

Pop Pop helped Daddy unload his mattresses in the living room. Daddy was such a skillful salesman that the mattresses seldom stayed there for more than a few days.

The last items unloaded from the truck were the bags of produce that Mama and Daddy picked up on their way to Hatteras at roadside stands in Terrell and Hyde counties. Typically, this included a few dozen ears of fresh corn and a quart of colorful, shelled butter beans. There were also a dozen tomatoes, some ripe and ready to be sliced. Those tomatoes, combined with bacon, lettuce, Duke's mayonnaise, and two slices of bread, made the best sandwich ever. The unripe ones were later battered, fried, and served as a sumptuous side dish at supper.

They also had a peck of peaches which we used to make homemade ice cream on Saturday night. Two cantaloupes and a watermelon rounded out the collection. I could hardly wait until the watermelon was chilled, sliced, and served. I agree with Mark Twain, who wrote, "When one has tasted watermelon, he knows what the angels eat." Watermelon was also Sister's fa-

Me and my brother Clifford, around 1955

vorite fruit. While most of us enjoyed only the seedless heart of the melon, she consumed it down to and including most of the rind.

Once the initial chaos of our parents' arrival faded, the whole family settled into the oversized rocking chairs or the swing on the pizer. The atmosphere was cheerful as my parents shared the latest news from Washington while relaxing and enjoying the cool ocean breeze. Meanwhile, Clifford and I competed for chances to tell our parents about our summer activities. I recounted my trips to the landing and Uncle Luther's house, while Clifford mainly focused on how Grandmom didn't allow him the freedom he felt he should have. Since our parents worked, we had less supervision in Washington than at Hatteras with Grandmom. She didn't work outside the home, so she could watch over us closely and she was a stricter disciplinarian than our parents. Due to his young age, Clifford struggled to adapt from his freedom in Washington to the more structured environment at Grandmom's house.

I was five and a half years older than my brother and took on a great deal of responsibility for his well-being in Washington while our parents were working. Whenever he misbehaved, I felt it was my duty to correct his poor judgment. I continued to bear this responsibility even when we were at Hatteras. What Grandmom didn't see him do, I often did. I'm sure I was as much a burden to him as she was because of my never-ending attempts to correct his behavior. Likewise, he was a burden to me as I felt obligated to take on the role of a surrogate parent. This was especially true when Daddy was drinking, and Mother was working her shift at the hospital.

Three days earlier, while running an errand to the store for Grandmom, my brother and one of his friends stepped onto the road from a side path right in front of me. They didn't realize I was behind them. If Clifford had known, he would have tossed aside the cigarette he was so boldly smoking as he approached the road. I had never smoked a cigarette, yet here was my eight-year-old brother puffing away like a pro. I knew our parents would disapprove, so I quickly moved closer to reprimand him. Before I could confront him, he spotted me out of the corner of his eye. Without missing a beat, he dropped the smoldering cigarette onto the sandy road and kept walking, staring straight ahead.

"Clifford," I asked, "what do you think you are doing?"

By this time, he was at least five steps ahead of where the cigarette had landed.

"What do you mean?" he said

"Smoking. I saw you smoking."

"I don't know what you're talking about," he said.

"I'll show you what I'm talking about," I said as I grabbed him by the shoulder, turned him around, and led him to the smoldering Lucky Strike lying on the sand.

"I saw you drop that cigarette right there." I pointed to the spot.

"What would Mama and Daddy think if they knew you were smoking?"

I thought that saying this would instill in him a fear of the Lord. Such an implied threat gave me power, allowing me to control his future behavior much more effectively.

"I didn't drop that cigarette," he proclaimed. "Somebody else must have dropped it."

I didn't say anything more about the smoking incident. In my adolescent mind, I thought I had scared my brother enough. I figured he would probably think twice before smoking again. I temporarily forgot about the incident the next day, but he hadn't. I must have made quite an impression on him when I asked, "What would Mama and Daddy think?" We both feared Daddy. He had convinced us that he would kill us in cold blood if we ever smoked cigarettes. It wasn't until we were much older that we learned his bark was far worse than his bite.

When there was a lull in the conversation on the pizer, Clifford dropped the bomb. With all the innocence of an angel that had just descended from Heaven, he turned to Daddy and said, "Daddy, I hate to tell you this, but Buddy has started smoking."

Daddy fell silent for a moment, absorbing what Clifford had just said. My heart stopped. He turned to me and calmly asked, "Son, is that true?"

I couldn't believe my ears as my brain struggled to process what was happening. Clifford had cleverly put me on the defensive with his lie. Daddy asked me if I had done something I knew I shouldn't do. The shock of the situation made my suntanned face turn a brilliant shade of red. I thought the capillaries in my face would dilate to the point of bursting, sending blood across the pizer. With such a guilty look, how could I convince anyone that my brother's recent accusation was false? I wanted to die on the spot, but not before taking care of Clifford.

"I ain't been smoking—he's the one who's been smoking!" I angrily replied, pointing a shaking finger at my brother as my adolescent voice cracked unpredictably between high-pitched squeaks and deep bass tones.

I felt like my response was so unconvincing that I was certain Daddy would see it as a desperate attempt to save myself. But all I could do was deny Clifford's fabricated story as I timidly pointed the finger of blame where it rightfully belonged. I am sure Daddy thought I was wrongfully accusing him of shifting the blame away from myself. I was sure a spanking awaited me for smoking and lying.

"I'd better not hear tell of you boys smoking," he said firmly. After a few more seconds of silence, the adults resumed their conversation, and the smoking issue was never mentioned again.

I will never know if he believed I was smoking, but I felt as guilty as if I had done it. Clifford had cleverly diffused what he thought would be his death sentence at my expense. He had no way of knowing that I had put the whole smoking incident to rest, at least when it came to telling Daddy. I knew that if Daddy found out, he would probably end up killing my brother. Since I didn't want him dead, snitching on him was not even an option; however, I didn't want him to realize that. As long as I kept the smoking incident from our parents, I assumed I had some control over his future behavior. All I had to do was threaten to tell on him, and he would do whatever I said. Who would have guessed that he, an eight-year-old boy, would be sneaky enough to strip me, a thirteen-year-old, of such power? I never underestimated his intelligence again.

Usually, the first week of Mama and Daddy's vacation was spent visiting relatives in the mornings, going to the beach after lunch, and stopping by the docks to buy fresh seafood to prepare for supper. Daddy played his banjo to entertain us in the evenings. Everyone seemed to enjoy this break from our usual routine back home.

After breakfast, a typical day began with everyone climbing into Daddy's truck to visit some of Mama's relatives. Riding in a vehicle was a special treat for my aunt and grandparents. Pop Pop owned only one car during his lifetime. He bought a second-hand vehicle for its engine, which he removed and installed in his boat. I don't recall him mentioning what he did with the rest of the car; he probably pushed it into a nearby creek, which was the fate of most rubbish back then.

Grandmom, dressed in a clean frock and bonnet, sat in the truck's cab with Daddy and Mama. Daddy had placed a bus seat in the truck's bed behind the cab, where Pop Pop, Sister, and I sat. Clifford perched on Pop Pop's lap. As we traveled slowly along the sandy ruts of the road, feeling the air rush by with mare's tail clouds lightly feathering against the brilliant blue Hatteras sky, I was confident that cruising in an expensive convertible would not have been any more thrilling.

Daddy would join us on some of our visits during the first week of my parents' vacation. However, most of the time, he would drop us off, go home to get some mattresses, and start knocking on the doors of potential customers. Since he wasn't available to pick us up after our visits, we walked back home with plenty of time for Grandmom to have dinner, our midday meal, ready on the table by 11:00 a.m.

After Mama woke from her usual after-dinner nap, everyone piled into Daddy's truck for a trip to the beach. I had always loved the beach, but didn't enjoy it as much when Grandmom came with us. Every time she joined us at the beach, she would tell the story of how, as a young girl, a wave knocked her down, swept her into the ocean, and she nearly drowned in a rip current. That experience left her terrified of the water. Grandmom passed that fear on to her daughters, who never learned to swim because Grandmom never allowed them deep enough into the water to practice. Although Mama was more relaxed about our playing in the water, my brother and I could never wade into the ocean past ankle-deep when Grandmom was around because she constantly reminded everyone of the dangers of the sea.

Daddy seldom stayed at the beach with us. He usually dropped us off at the beach next to the Atlantic View Hotel, across the road from The Beacon, a local bar that sold beer. We walked the rest of the way across the scorching sand under the summer sun to the refreshing Atlantic surf.

The few times Daddy took us to the beach, we rarely stayed longer than fifteen minutes. He never owned a bathing suit, so his outfit for an afternoon at the beach was completely unsuitable. Daddy wore his felt hat, long pants, and a dress shirt. He removed his shoes and socks, revealing incredibly pale feet that had never seen the light of a sunny day. After a few minutes of wading with his pant legs rolled up above his knees, he declared he didn't like "all that damn sand between his toes." When he announced it was time to leave, no one argued because we understood that asking to stay would be pointless.

When he wasn't with us, we had more time to enjoy the beach. However, around 3:00 p.m., we began the long walk home so Grandmom and Mama could start supper.

Supper was always special when Mama was in Hatteras. We rarely had seafood without my parents since Grandmom never strayed from her usual menu of eggs, bacon, yeast rolls, and jelly. Instead, Mama prepared more culinary delights, like fried or baked fish, shrimp, oysters, and hard- and soft-shell crabs. When paired with the fresh produce that my parents brought from the mainland, our suppers would make Julia Child turn green with envy.

Grandmom gave Mama free rein in the kitchen. After caring for my brother and me all summer, she felt she deserved a vacation. However, that doesn't mean Grandmom stayed out of the kitchen during meal preparations. Although she let Mama cook, Grandmom took on the role of supervisor.

Mama fried seafood better than anyone else in the world. Her shrimp and crabs were bites of heaven—sweeter than candy. To this day, I've never tasted fried shrimp that comes close to hers. When it came to seafood, she was a culinary master.

After the first week of vacation, Daddy had sold all his mattresses. He grew restless and bored. His lack of imagination for something more engaging led him to The Beacon, one of two "beer joints" on the island's southern end. He spent his mattress profits on beer there. Sometimes, he found someone to sell him whiskey, even though it was not legally available for sale on the island at the time.

Daddy drank heavily and stayed drunk for the entire second week of my parents' vacation until his money ran out. After that, he drank anything with alcohol in it. One night, Mama had to ask Uncle Luther, a neighbor across the road, to take him to Buxton, where the only doctor on the island lived. Daddy had drunk his shaving lotion, the only liquid he could find in the house with alcohol in it. After the doctor pumped his stomach, they brought him back home to sober up.

His addiction was a significant embarrassment for Mama and also humiliating for my brother and me. However, it never seemed to agitate Grandmom, Pop Pop, or Sister. If it did, they never let it show. They always treated Daddy with kindness and respect.

It wasn't until I was an adult that I fully understood that alcoholism was a disease. By then, the damage had already been done. Like many children of alcoholics, my brother and I carry the emotional scars from growing up in that environment. Mama, my brother, and I lived in a constant state of tension, always wondering when the next drinking binge would start, where our next meal would come from, or if we'd have a roof over our heads. The uncertainty was relentless, weighing heavily on us every day. Despite this, we had a lifeline: Mama. She taught us how to face adversity with strength and resilience. She frequently reminded us of the dangers of alcohol and other drugs. Equally important, she gave us summers at Hatteras with her parents, where we could let the gentle summer breezes blow away the cobwebs of having a drug-dependent parent from our minds, allowing us to be carefree kids if only for a few weeks out of the year.

CHAPTER 13

Going Visiting

As a child, one of my favorite pastimes was visiting the residents of Hatteras. We went visiting all summer, not just when my parents were there. I am always fascinated by the diverse and vibrant personalities of this small community. What stands out most about the village natives is their deep-rooted acceptance and patience for each other's individuality. Everyone has a place in this close-knit community regardless of differences. To this day, neighbors readily support each other in times of need. I take great pride in being related to many of these remarkable people.

One such person was Mama's first cousin, Moody. He lived in the village his whole life, except for a few years spent working on a dredge in Norfolk. For most of his seventy years, his primary source of income was clamming. He sold his daily catch to a local fish house, which paid him just a penny per clam. Moody's favorite spot for catching those tasty bivalves was the shallow shoals near Hatteras Inlet.

The only motorized vehicle he ever owned was his flat-bottom, sixteen-foot boat with an air-cooled engine. For him, wading through the shallow flats and trudging along the sandy paths and unpaved village roads was always challenging due to a deformity on his left side. A congenital disability affected his arm and leg. He never let that hold him back because when he wasn't clamming, Moody was busy building model boats from juniper and other materials he found along the shores of the sound. It was a challenging hobby due to his withered arm, but he never let that stop him. When tourists

Cousin Dezzie and Victoria Austin's house

first started visiting the island, he was one of the early artisans of the village. His talent helped supplement his modest income.

My grandparents were poor, but compared to Moody, they seemed wealthy. Moody's life was one of existence without any frills. His disadvantaged lifestyle gave me my first close-up glimpse of real poverty. Like his home, he was somewhat disheveled. He was a short, slender man who appeared somewhat undernourished. Seeing him wearing the same tattered clothes for several days was not unusual. His long white hair and beard framed a tanned, wrinkled, weather-beaten face, with eyes that, behind thick glasses with scratched lenses and broken black plastic frames, expressed his soul's gentle, kind, and warm-hearted nature. He lived in a Bohemian style reminiscent of the 1960s, twenty years ahead of its time. Moody was a gentle spirit and a soft-spoken man whose accent unmistakably revealed him as a native Hatteras man. Moody first made me realize that a person's appear-

Moody's model wooden schooner

ance, education, or wealth isn't what truly matters; instead, it's the spirit that resides within an individual that counts.

Moody and his family often appeared on my mother's list of people to visit when she came to Hatteras. I was always excited to accompany her. Moody lived in a small, unadorned wooden house. Its peeling paint bore witness to years of wear. The plastic shades at the windows were lowered, blocking most of the sunlight. The living room's dark walls loomed like storm clouds, casting shadows over the somber atmosphere. Old quilts were draped over the worn sofa and chairs, clinging to them like autumn leaves unwilling to let go. Moody's frail wife, Ruth, was typically lying on the couch during our visits. She would rise just long enough to wrap us in a warm embrace before sinking back into her sofa, where she held court, detailing her ailments with the precision of a seasoned storyteller, ensuring no ache or ailment went unmentioned throughout our visit. Scattered papers and magazines layered the room in quiet chaos as if the space had been collecting memories in print. Cats and kittens drifted in and out like restless spirits, slipping through doorways from the kitchen and porches. Overhead, a bare light bulb swayed gently from a short, exposed wire.

On the dark gray wall opposite the sofa, hung a large picture of Jesus kneeling in prayer in the Garden of Gethsemane. A brilliant ray of light pierced through the clouds in the upper left corner of the painting, bathing Jesus in a bright glow. It was the only bright spot in the room. For Moody, the picture depicted a divine promise, a reminder that one day he would exchange his earthly poverty for streets of gold.

At the end of our visit, Moody insisted on taking us to the shed behind his house where he kept his model boats. Without any assistance, he dragged his left foot as he made his way to the rickety old shed. The building stood out more in respect for Moody than for its structural integrity. Lined up along the inside back wall, much like the fence pickets in front of the old Durant Lifesaving station, were a dozen two- and three-mast model schooners measuring twelve to twenty-four inches long. The gleam in his eyes reflected the pride in his handiwork.

Moody was resourceful in acquiring the materials to build his schooners. He used old twine for the rigging, which he collected along the shore after fishermen had discarded it while they were repairing their nets. He painted the models with leftover paint from cans that local villagers had thrown away. His only investment in these unique replicas was his time.

He sold the smaller vessels for $7 and the larger ones for $14. One of Moody's model ships still rests on a table in Grandmom's old house. It was a gift from Moody to my grandparents, who always offered him food whenever he unexpectedly, yet not surprisingly, dropped by for a meal. Worried that his home wouldn't withstand a hurricane's fury, he sought shelter with them whenever storms battered the delicate ribbon of sand known as the Outer Banks.

Mama always tried to fit in two visits during her morning outings. Since it was a short walk from Moody's house to the main road where several of Mama's cousins lived, she suggested we go there next. I especially enjoyed visiting Dezzie, Victoria, and Garland. We could always count on the two sisters to be home. They led a very sheltered life. However, we rarely found their brother Garland there since he was usually away working on a dredge in Florida. Garland and Dezzie never walked down the aisle, but Victoria did—though her marriage lasted barely longer than the ceremony. She spent one night as a wife, and by morning, she was back home, leaving behind whispers and speculation. Whatever drove her swift return remains a mystery, shrouded in the shadows of a marriage that never truly began. Afterward, the two sisters seldom left home. Before Victoria's marriage, the sisters socialized like all the other natives, participating in church activities, social events, and visiting relatives and friends. No family member ever discussed the details of Victoria's failed marriage. However, its impact changed the lives of these three siblings forever.

Victoria left home only to visit the grocery store and the post office. Dezzie never ventured out. Garland took on the role of breadwinner, providing their only source of income. His effort to offer them modern conveniences was never appreciated.

He wired the house for electricity, yet they clung to the kerosene lamps. In a rare concession, they accepted a radio—but only on their terms, plugging it in just long enough to hear the news, as if afraid an unseen current might seep into their way of life. Every appliance Garland introduced was dutifully unplugged by his sisters the moment he left for work, and it was as if his efforts to illuminate their world flickered out the second he walked out the door.

He purchased a television in the early 1960s and installed a large antenna adjacent to the house. This antenna would sometimes, on clear nights, receive broadcasts from the nearest stations, which were no closer than one hundred miles away. He believed this modern marvel would entertain his reclusive sisters, but that was not the case. When he left home to return to work in Florida, they unplugged the TV and stored it under the stairs in the hallway.

We approached their home along a winding trail that branched off a short side road connected to the village's main sandy street. The path had the appearance of a time tunnel, transporting visitors to a bygone era. Their house was encircled by a thicket of live oaks, myrtles, and yaupons, resembling the walls of a fort, designed to shield this isolated sanctuary from the influences of the present. Garland planted a coconut palm tree from Florida in the front yard, where it grew like an out-of-place visitor, its tropical form stark against the local greenery. The small, weathered white house sat in an unkept yard, its clapboard siding chipped and faded from years of withstanding storms. The house appeared hollow and forgotten. It had remained unchanged since

Dezzie and Victoria's birdhouses

their childhood in the early 1900s, as if time had abandoned it to decay in silence. It was the home where these siblings were born and raised and where
the sisters spent their entire lives. Only the upstairs bedroom windows and
the kitchen windows downstairs had screens attached to their lower halves
to keep the insects out. Layers of thick, lead-based paint sealed all the other
windows shut.

Behind the kitchen stood a large red brick cistern connected by downspouts to the gutters along the house's roof. The family graveyard was approximately twenty-five feet from the side porch that led into the kitchen.
A retaining wall of concrete blocks enclosed the small cemetery. Garland
brought some sand from the beach and placed it inside the wall, raising the
land's elevation several feet higher than the rest of the yard. This prevented
storm tides that typically flooded the yard from covering the graves of their
parents.

Several small pie pans filled with water rested on the retaining wall. Dezzie
and Victoria, both birdwatchers at heart, had placed them there to serve as
birdbaths, creating a tiny oasis in the stillness. They took great joy in telling
us about the birds that came to drink and splash near the birdfeeder.

A thicket of live oaks shaded the retaining wall surrounding the graveyard. Several petunia plants with slender, delicate yellow-green stems and

leaves reached desperately toward brighter light as they grew beside the shaded border, filling the surrounding area with a sweet fragrance.

We walked into the yard, stepped up on the side porch, and knocked on the kitchen door. Victoria answered the door and greeted us with a pleasant smile. She was wearing a knee-length cotton dress that buttoned in the front. The fabric was limp from years of wear and washing, clinging to her thin frame like a wilted flower.

"My blessed, look who is here!" she exclaimed.

As we entered the kitchen, she hugged us and then escorted us to an adjacent small room that served as a dining and sitting room.

A kettle whistled on the kerosene cookstove in the kitchen, adding to the suffocating humidity of an already sweltering day. The sharp fumes from the burning fuel merged with the steam rising from the kettle, thickening the air until it felt like the room was breathing in the heat.

A can of meat and vegetables, the day's lunch, sat on the counter near the water bucket. Years ago, Garland had plumbed the house with running water from the cistern. But the sisters' habit was to go outside and scoop water into a bucket from an opening on top of the cistern. Together, they would bring the heavy bucket into the house.

Dezzie and Victoria only ate canned foods bought from Mr. Dan's general store, where their parents had always shopped. Victoria only trusted the food sold there. She and Dezzie were wary that someone might slip poison into food that wasn't in a can; therefore, fresh produce and meat were never part of their diet. They consumed nothing Garland brought into the house unless he guaranteed he had purchased it at Mr. Dan's store.

Everyone sat in the wooden, straight-back dining chairs Victoria had placed around the room's edge, their stillness contrasting with her hurried footsteps as she dashed down the hallway toward the front of the house, passing the forgotten TV tucked under the stairs. She paused at the base of the stairs, near the rarely opened front door, as if the threshold held some silent significance. Holding onto the newel post that supported the banister, she yelled up the stairwell, "Dezzie, come on down. Naomi, Buddy, Sissy, and Essie are here." She always called Pop Pop "Buddy" and Grandmom "Sissy." They were her uncle and aunt; consequently, my aunt and Mama were their cousins.

Victoria returned to the room where we were sitting. Before taking a seat, she tried to get Grandmom to switch from the straight-backed dining room chair in which she was sitting to one of the two unoccupied wooden rocking chairs. Victoria said it would be more comfortable. Grandmom assured her that she was satisfied with where she was. Victoria sat in the rocking chair, where she always perched when visitors were not around. The other rocker was Dezzie's.

Victoria was a gracious hostess. Cheerful and sincere, she asked us what we had been doing since she last saw us. The room was filled with chatter in the old Hatteras dialect as the relatives updated each other on events since they had last been together. A genuine atmosphere of love and concern permeated the room.

Fifteen minutes passed before Dezzie came down from upstairs, where she had been in her bedroom. As she walked into the room, she threw both hands in the air, grinned from ear to ear, and exclaimed as if she didn't know we were there, "My blessed, look who's here!" Right away, her voice dropped in volume as she apologetically added, "Young'uns, you'll have to forgive me for not coming down right away, but I was taking a bath."

The hugging scene at the kitchen door with Victoria played out again in the sitting room with Dezzie. Before Dezzie sat down, mimicking her sister's mannerisms and dialogue, she offered the remaining rocking chair to Grandmom. Again, Grandmom politely declined and insisted she was just fine.

Dezzie, the taller of the two sisters, wore a faded cotton frock made from the material of feedbags that once held corn for the chickens. The dress was at least twenty-five years old.

Neither sister wore makeup. Dezzie's hair was pulled back and twisted into a bun at the nape of her neck. There was a dark brown growth on her upper right cheek, about the size of a man's thumb, protruding approximately two inches from her face. It looked pretty painful and grotesque as it dangled from her cheek. When Mama expressed concern, Dezzie told us, "Every so often, it falls off, but it grows right back again."

"You should let a doctor look at it," Mama said, worried that her cousin may have cancer.

"Why honey," Dezzie replied, "it ain't nothing but a seed wart of some kind of another. One of these days, it will fall off, and the Lord willing, it ain't never going to grow back."

Mama chose to drop the issue since they disregarded her advice. She knew Dezzie wouldn't leave home anyway. Dezzie hadn't stepped outside the yard for years since Victoria came home the morning after her wedding. Mama understood that it would take more than a "seed wart" to make her leave. Seeing a doctor was out of the question.

Garland desperately tried to get his sisters to visit their neighbors and family, but they would not yield. Although they were always friendly to those who visited them, they refused to return the favor.

Both sisters enjoyed discussing the past and often steered the conversation in that direction. It typically focused on their family life before Victoria's marriage. No one ever mentioned that incident. The talks primarily focused on "the good old days" when their parents were alive. I loved hearing their stories about their "poppie" and "mommie" as much as they loved sharing them. Dezzie's memories were more serious, while Victoria's were livelier and more humorous.

As 10:30 a.m. approached, Grandmom grew restless. She said it was time for us to head home. She preferred to serve dinner at 11:00 a.m., not a minute earlier or later. We knew we would delay dinner because we had to walk home, about half a mile, along a deep, sandy road.

"Why young'uns, there is no need for you to go. Why don't you stay and eat with us?" Dezzie politely begged as we made our way to the door.

"Merciful fathers, honey, I couldn't eat a mou'ful if I had to," Grandmom responded. "Besides, we need to get back up the road."

I was sure Grandmom lied about not being hungry because she didn't like eating at someone else's home. Even if we had accepted their polite invitation, the two cans on the kitchen counter contained only enough food for a couple of people. Both sisters gave us a big goodbye hug as we walked outside. Before following us on the porch, both sisters covered their heads with old-fashioned sunbonnets that hung from a nail by the back door. It was obvious from their pale skin that Dezzie and Victoria were not sun worshipers. Looking much like subjects in an old tin-type photograph, they stood on the porch and watched as we made our way from their yard down the path that emptied us back into the present and onto the road that led to Grandmom's house.

On the way home, I asked Grandmom what a maful was. She said it was slang for a mouthful. "Oh, yeah? I thought it was something that Dezzie and Victoria were fixing for dinner," I declared.

After Grandmom and Pop Pop passed away, I continued to visit their nieces. Seeing them was as enjoyable as watching a rerun of a favorite old

Graves of the three Austin siblings

movie. Whenever I visited, Victoria greeted me at the kitchen door with her big smile and a warm hug. She always escorted me to the sitting room, past the burning kerosene fumes, and through the humid kitchen. Two cans of food always sat near the water bucket, waiting to be warmed up and served for the next meal. Across the room was the kerosene cookstove next to a more modern gas range, which Garland purchased for her and Dezzie in the 1960s. The sisters never used the gas stove, so it remained as grease-free as the day it was brought into the house.

Victoria yelled at Dezzie from the base of the stairs, saying I was there. After at least fifteen minutes, she descended from her bedroom. No matter what time of day I visited, she always used the excuse of "taking a bath" for not coming immediately. The "seed wart" had recently fallen off her cheek, leaving a pink scar.

Our conversation, filled with laughter and concern for family, drifted through the windows and the back door, eventually fading into the delightful ocean breeze outside. After our visit, they followed me to the back porch and watched as I disappeared down the path. This path, even today, remains a route that shuttles between the past and the present.

After many years, I returned to visit one morning. Everything still looked the same, except for the three newly erected tombstones in the higher part of the yard, nestled among the crumbling concrete blocks of the cemetery's moss-covered retaining wall. Garland and his two sisters lie buried beside each other near their "mommie" and "poppie." Like the palm tree in the front yard, the new granite headstones seem out of place amid the surrounding old maritime thicket. The pale lavender petunias continued to fill the air with their sweet fragrance as they stretched from the shade toward a sunny spot in the yard.

In the solitude beside their graves, where a low roar of the ocean could be heard, I updated Mama's cousins on the latest chapter in the family history. Mama and her sister had passed away recently, and I knew their cousins would want to know.

CHAPTER 14

Going to Supper

My grandparents could not afford upholstered furniture—only straight-backed wooden chairs and rockers. On the southwest side of the sitting room were two timeworn, high-backed rocking chairs—their favorites. Each chair occupied a space beside one of two separate windows, allowing the evening sun's winter rays to shine through and warm them. At the same time, the summer breeze cooled them when the windows were open. By now, the clear varnish that highlighted the wood grain of the chairs had taken on an orange tint. The armrests had darkened from years of sweat and dirt accumulated from their arms and hands. For Grandmom, this was a place to rest and hum a favorite old hymn or read the Bible; for Pop Pop, it was a spot to daydream and chew a plug of Apple Tobacco. He told me he began chewing when his grandfather gave him a small taste at the age of three. At ninety-three, he died in his chair with a cake of tobacco in his flannel shirt pocket—the arms of the chair, like a mother's longing embrace, held his slumped, lifeless body until the undertakers arrived.

During the daylight hours of the warm months, my grandparents would move these chairs from the sitting room to the pizer to accommodate family visitors and then back to their usual place in the evenings. I was rocking on the pizer, waiting to be called in for supper, while the aroma of shrimp frying in the kitchen teased my nostrils. Grandmom poked her head out the front door and announced in her usual stern yet loving way, "All hands, come on in for supper. Now, don't waste a minute. It's on the table, and it's getting cold." I had been waiting to hear her say those words since we'd left

Mama and Grandmom cooking

Washington that morning for a weekend visit to Hatteras with my grandparents and aunt.

The timing of our visit was perfect. My brother and I had a day off from school, and Mama wanted to enjoy a long weekend away from her job at the hospital. We left home early, around 6:00 a.m. The drive to Grandma's house at Hatteras took the entire day. Although the trip was only 173 miles long, the need to take three ferries complicated it: one at Alligator River, another at Mann's Harbor, where we crossed Croatan Sound, and a third at Oregon Inlet, adding at least three extra hours to our travel time, making the journey rather exhausting.

Catching the ferry was seldom about perfect timing. More often than not, it felt like waiting for a slow-motion pendulum to swing back in our favor. We would usually arrive at the docks just in time to see the ferry depart, leaving us idling in a long queue of cars, each patiently waiting for its return. Sometimes, we would watch the ferry complete several cycles—coming and going, coming and going—before our turn arrived. The ramp on the front of the ferry finally lowered in front of us, a long-awaited invitation for us to board.

Crossing Oregon Inlet feels like shedding a heavy cloak and stepping into the sunlight. As a child, I didn't understand why my spirit soared when we rolled onto Hatteras Island—it simply did. Now I see it. Oregon Inlet is more than just a stretch of water; it's a gateway, a bridge from the weight of the world to the lightness of freedom. Like a seabird catching the wind, I—and countless others—feel our burdens lifted the moment we arrive. Recently, I asked a good friend who moved to Hatteras to escape the frustrations of corporate life to share what makes the island unique to him. He quoted an inscription on a plaque his mother had placed on the wall in their island home.

Here, time is slow and gracious,
 A companion, not a master.

Those words perfectly capture the allure of Hatteras. This seductiveness attracts many people to her waters, bathing them in serenity.

It was mid-September 1956. The air on the island lacked the humidity typically associated with August and early September. With its razor-sharp crispness, a gentle breeze from the north reminded us that fall was approaching. The cloudless sky, dotted with monarch butterflies on their annual migration to Mexico, provided further evidence that fall was just days away. Mama, my brother, and I traveled south to my grandparents' home, accompanied by the butterflies.

My excitement grew as we approached Grandmom's house. I couldn't wait to return to Hatteras Village. Mama's big smile reflected her enthusiasm, too. She told us she had heard the shrimpers were "pulling in record catches, and, if the Lord is willing," she would prepare some for supper. Shrimp was Mama's favorite seafood.

We arrived at Grandmom's house late in the afternoon. After a brief visit with my grandparents and aunt, we all piled into the car and headed to Oden's fish house. If shrimp were available on the island, we could typically buy them there.

We turned off the main road beside Mr. Dan's store onto a single-lane road of oyster shells that led to the fish house. As Mama parked the car, we spotted a shrimp boat unloading its catch at the wharf. A faint stench of decaying sea life permeated the air. Its source was the wharf in front of the fish house. The daily buildup of slime from the fish and shrimp unloaded by local fishermen's trawlers and skiffs onto the dock was impossible to wash away. The air, ever so slightly tainted, carried whispers of yesterday's catch, a reminder that the sea gives, but never without leaving its mark.

Local boys, barefoot and shirtless, gathered on the dock before the fish house. They squatted beside mounds of shrimp that several trawlers had offloaded. Six hours earlier, those flavorful crustaceans had been swimming and scavenging at the bottom of Pamlico Sound. With impressive speed, the boys picked up a shrimp in each hand, forced their thumbs between the head and body, and sent the animal's head flying off with a quick flick of their thumbs, landing in a growing pile near their feet. Without pausing, they grabbed another shrimp and repeated the process. When their hands were so full that they could no longer hold any more of the decapitated shrimp bodies, the young workers tossed them into wire baskets the fish house owner provided. This pick—flick-fly-toss rhythm continued until all the shrimp were beheaded. Once weighed, they were packed on ice inside wooden rectangular boxes, loaded onto a local freight boat, and sent to seafood distributors on the mainland. There's a technique to "heading shrimp," as it is called, and every boy on the dock was a master of this skill. They earned two cents a pound for their efforts. When they separated the last head from the shrimp's body, some guys could earn as much as ten dollars. It was not a bad day's work for teenage boys living in Hatteras Village in the fifties.

"Hey, Donald. How ya doing?" Mama asked the fish house owner, who was busy weighing fish that Mr. Nacie, a local pound net fisherman, was selling to him.

"Why hey, Naomi," Donald responded, looking away from the large set of scales where Mr. Nacie weighed his fish.

"Me and the boys, we drove here today. I heard that the shrimpers were doing really good this season, and by the looks of things, the rumor is true."

"My blessed, I ain't never seen so many as we've had this season," responded Donald. "Do you want a mess of them?"

"I sure do. I was hoping I was going to be able to have some for supper. Weigh me out about three pounds."

As Donald packaged the shrimp for Mama, Grandmom noticed several porgies lying in the stern of Mr. Nacie's skiff. She walked to the edge of the dock, where the boat was tied, to get a better look at a fish she dearly loved to eat.

While Mr. Nacie shoveled fish from the skiff onto the dock, he spotted Grandmom eyeing the porgies.

"Maggie, how'd you like one of these porgies to bake for supper?" he said.

"Why, Nacie, that sure would be nice. Are you sure you can spare one?"

"Now you know there is more here than I can eat," replied Mr. Nacie.

As was customary for the watermen of that time, they offered fish free to residents. The people of Hatteras looked out for one another. If a local wanted a mess of fish, they needed to arrive at the docks when the fishermen returned with their catch. They exchanged money for fish only when they shipped it off the island.

"Why Nacie, honey, I sure do appreciate that," expressed Grandmom, whose face was beaming. She called everybody honey.

"Clifford," she shouted to my grandfather, who was paying for the shrimp just inside the fish house door, "look at what Nacie's done and give us."

She held up the porgy so all of us could see it.

"My blessed, Nacie, you didn't have to do that," responded Pop Pop.

"It is my pleasure," responded Mr. Nacie as he tossed another shovel full of fish from his skiff up on the dock.

"I'll clean it for Mag to bake for supper tomorrow night. Much obliged!" my grandfather shouted as he ambled from the docks toward the car.

We drove home with plenty of fresh seafood for two suppers: fried shrimp tonight and baked porgy tomorrow night.

Pop Pop cleaned the porgy by the pond next to the house on a makeshift table he built from a board and some cement blocks. He removed the scales and guts, tossing them into the pond. He left the head attached to the fish's body. After making several vertical slits along its side, he placed the porgy in the icebox until Grandmom could bake it for Saturday night. At that time, we still referred to the refrigerator as an icebox, a throwback to when electricity was unavailable in the village. Even today, I find myself calling that kitchen appliance an icebox. Some habits are hard to break.

Meanwhile, Grandmom helped Mama clean the shrimp and wash them in a pan of water on the kitchen table. Because Grandmom's kitchen lacked counters, the table was used for food preparation and dining. Mama carefully removed the black veins from the backs of the shrimp, explaining that this dark substance was the shrimp's intestine and contents which she called shrimp hockey and said she didn't want us to eat it. My mother, being a nurse, was very conscious of cleanliness.

Once the shrimp were deveined and thoroughly rinsed, Grandmom rolled them in a dry mixture of flour, salt, and pepper. Mama melted several tablespoons of lard in a cast-iron skillet, blackened and crusty from years of use. When the shrimp hit the hot grease, moisture from these succulent crustaceans reacted with the lard, sending blistering beads of grease flying from the pan. After sending the critters to their sizzling fate, Mama hastily jumped back from the stove to avoid burns. Every so often, while the shrimp cooked, it was not unusual to hear a few of Mama's sporadic high-pitched yelps from the kitchen as the spattering grease struck her skin. Often, she held a pot lid near the skillet to protect herself from the painful droplets. She reminded me of a gladiator defending himself from the dangers lurking beyond his shield.

As the shrimp turned pale pink, Mama carefully flipped them over using a long-handled fork. After turning the last shrimp, she covered the sizzling morsels with a lid. They remained on the heat until the light flour coating turned a golden amber. Then, she transferred the shrimp to a bowl she covered with an old, dented aluminum lid, its matching pot having long since been discarded. She continued this routine until she had cooked all the shrimp.

Grandmom made her famous pan-fried cornbread fritters to accompany the shrimp while Mama prepared the coleslaw. My aunt, who never claimed to be a cook, set the table with the dishes and flatware. She also placed a container of King Por-T-Rik molasses in the center of the table. Cornbread fritters drenched in molasses were our dessert.

Everyone in the family loved shrimp, and it didn't take us long to eat a heaping platter of them. I quickly ate my share of shrimp and then used the old "Bruno" tactic to snag my aunt's portion.

When my aunt and Mama were children, a fisherman named Bruno lived in the community. One day, he sailed out into the sound to check his nets and fell overboard, drowning in the process. When he did not return to the landing that evening, a search party set out to find him. They found his boat tied to his net stakes, but they didn't discover his body until three days later. That afternoon, a local search party puttered into the harbor, towing Bruno's body behind them. News of his fate spread through the village like wildfire. Curious onlookers, including my aunt, rushed to the landing to catch a glimpse of the situation. Bruno was floating, secured to the boat with a rope tied around one of his legs. Shrimp clung to his exposed flesh, making him look like a creature from the deep. A tragic scene of this kind was the first time my aunt had witnessed a drowning victim, and she had no idea that shrimp are scavengers that feed on dead organic matter. From that moment on, shrimp were officially off her menu—until middle age, when she ultimately convinced herself to give them another try. Even then, all it took was someone casually mentioning Bruno at the dinner table to make her push her plate away and suddenly remember she wasn't that hungry.

She really should've kept that story to herself. After all, there was no turning back once I discovered that simply saying "Bruno" could magically make her plate of shrimp slide my way. I ate hers more slowly than my own, savoring every crispy bite with the smug satisfaction of a guiltless hustler. Today, I feel somewhat ashamed of my childish trickery, but to be honest, I mostly remember how incredibly delicious those shrimp tasted.

The following evening, Grandmom prepared the porgy by placing the fish in a large baking pan and covering it with chopped onions, potatoes, and plenty of salt and pepper. She baked it in the oven. When it was time to serve, Grandmom arranged the porgy on a large platter alongside the onions and potatoes. To complete the dish, she poured the juices that remained in the pan over the porgy, giving it a final touch that made it resemble something from the finest restaurants.

Only my aunt felt ill when someone mentioned Bruno's name. However, Grandmom could make us quite queasy when she served baked porgy. I will never forget how I felt the first time I saw her eat it.

The family served themselves generous portions of flaky white meat from the sides of the fish and covered them in steaming onions and potatoes. Everyone, that is, except Grandmom! She placed the fish's head on her plate. She faced no competition from her family for that particular part of the fish. I watched as she delicately carved into the fish's face, savoring every morsel like an artist chiseling fine details into a sculpture. But when she casually popped one of its eyes into her mouth, I couldn't believe my eyes. She chewed it first on one side of her mouth, then on the other, carefully avoiding the hidden hard lens. It was clear from her expressions that she enjoyed this unusual delicacy. Watching her eat the fish head had already set my stomach doing somersaults. Still, when she casually spat the lens onto her plate like it was an olive pit—only to pop the other eye into her mouth—I was seconds away from losing my supper.

I thought, "Now, I've read in *National Geographic* that Arabs eat sheep eyes. But I've never heard of anyone eating fish eyes. Lord have mercy, how could she do that!"

From that time on, whenever she served baked porgy, I tried not to watch her eat the eyes, yet I wrestled with my curiosity about wanting to see her do it. Saturday night, she did not disappoint me. She ate the eyes of Mr. Nacie's porgy with the same gusto I had seen her do many times before.

Our visit ended Sunday morning. It was time to head home, which meant retracing the travel events of the previous Friday, but this time in reverse order. Unlike our journey north to Oregon Inlet, the monarch butterflies were migrating south, making their way to Mexico.

We arrived at the ferry just as the fully loaded vessel was leaving the dock. Forty-two cars lined up in front of us, so we waited at least an hour before the shuttle took us across Oregon Inlet. My brother and I took advantage of the extra time to explore the nearby beach and dunes. As I walked to the beach, visions of mouth-watering golden shrimp and delicious baked porgy danced through my mind. I could almost taste them.

Mama sat in the car, a gentle breeze from the ocean flowing through her curly black hair as she read a romance novel, smiling at each word.

We boarded the ferry all too soon to cross Oregon Inlet, leaving behind our gentle companion—*slow and gracious time.* On the other side, we stepped back into a fast-paced world where time was no longer *a friend but a master* urging us onward.

CHAPTER 15

Going to Heaven

By midafternoon, the house settled into its quiet rhythm. Aunt Essie—who I called Sister—was busy at Mr. Dolph's store and wouldn't return until the old clock on the sideboard struck five. Until then, Grandmom and Pop Pop had only each other for company. Like clockwork, this hour was when Mary would stop by. Mary was my grandmother's niece and the daughter of Grandmom's sister who lived across the street. Her daily visit was a steady thread woven into the fabric of their routine.

Shortly after her husband passed away, Mary had moved back to Hatteras, tore down her dilapidated childhood home, and built a new house with her husband's insurance money. The new house faced directly across the road from Grandmom and Pop Pop's home. Returning to Hatteras filled Mary with joy, offering a welcome escape from the fast-paced life in New Jersey. Surrounded by family whose familiar faces had shaped her childhood, she felt an undeniable sense of comfort and belonging. Although both her parents had passed away, two of her father's brothers and their wives lived on either side of her. At the same time, two other widowed aunts resided behind her on a short, dead-end path beside her yard.

Mary felt a profound sense of purpose when she visited Pop Pop and Grandmom, her mother's only surviving sister. She could value their company while looking after their well-being, and she anticipated it eagerly. This was the second time she had crossed the road today to check on her Aunt Mag and Uncle Clifford.

An enjoyable April day wrapped the world in warmth, whispering that

Grandmom and Pop Pop on the pizer

spring had finally arrived. The air was still, undisturbed, and peaceful. She noticed that the two doors at the front of the house stood open, and the windows were raised for the first time since last fall as if the house were taking its first deep breath after a long hibernation. As she raised her hand to knock on the screen door leading from the pizer into the sitting room, she heard the tune of a familiar hymn floating from inside to the pizer. It was as if angels were singing inside.

Precious memories, how they linger,
How they ever flood my soul . . .

She paused momentarily, considering that it might be the radio or television she heard. However, both devices were in the sitting room, and the music came from another room. Quietly, she opened the screen door and stepped inside.

In the stillness of midnight
Precious sacred scenes unfold . . .

My grandmom's niece Mary, who cared for my
grandparents during their later years

Mary followed the sound of the music, her footsteps light as she passed
through the doorway, down the hall, and into the only bedroom on the first
floor. There, in the soft afternoon light, Grandmom lay in a hospice-provided
bed, its head raised so that she was upright. Pop Pop sat beside her, his chair
drawn near as if closing the space between them could prevent time from
pulling them apart. Her long, wispy white hair, usually woven into a neat
plait and pinned securely, now spilled freely over the pillow like strands of
silver. Pop Pop leaned in, cradling her frail right hand against his face, as she

gazed at him with hazel eyes filled with quiet tenderness—a lifetime of love captured in a single glance.

Precious memories, unseen angels
Sent from somewhere to my soul.
How they linger ever near me
Heaven's sacred paths unfold.

Mary hesitated, rooted in place, unsure whether she was intruding on a rare, sacred moment between them. Grandmom's decline was a painful echo of her mother's before her, first revealing itself when a series of mini strokes struck at eighty-one. Since then, dementia had slowly robbed her of the essentials of her existence—her ability to recognize family, make sense of her surroundings, walk, talk, or even sense when she needed the bathroom. She had not uttered a word for several days. Grandmom's voice seemed lost in the silence of her illness. And yet, here she was, singing—her frail voice steady, recalling every lyric of her favorite hymn as if time had momentarily loosened its grip . . .

Precious memories, how they linger,
How they ever flood my soul . . .

. . . as she gazed at the light of her life, the man with whom she had spent nearly seventy years, their rich and pure voices intertwined like an angel's song, each note a testament to their deep affection for one another. As they looked into each other's eyes, their expressions conveyed the passion and tenderness of newlyweds exchanging vows at the altar. Together, they transformed the old hymn, blending their distinct voices into perfect harmony, much like the unique qualities each brought to their marriage—complementing, enriching, and strengthening the bond they had built over a lifetime.

In the stillness of the midnight
Precious sacred scenes unfold.

Without making a sound to avoid disturbing them, Mary turned and left her ailing aunt and uncle alone to enjoy each other's company. She had never witnessed such a profound expression of love or devotion. She could not hold back her tears as their voices faded behind her.

As the final notes of the hymn faded, Grandmom's breathing grew shallow, and her eyes drifted into the distant gaze they had worn for weeks. A quiet stillness settled over Grandmom as if the world beyond her were slipping further away. Grandmom, surrounded by the unfamiliar stillness of the room, stared vacantly at the tear-streaked face of the man holding her hand, her connection to the world quietly receding.

Pop Pop sat motionless, the moment's weight settling over him like a precious, unspoken gift. He closed his eyes, his heart full of gratitude, and bowed his head in silent prayer, thanking God for the rare blessing he had just experienced. As he did, his thoughts drifted back through the corridors of time to June 13, 1903—seventy years earlier—when the foundation of his life, his love, and his purpose was first laid. He told us the story many times.

A light sow-westerly wind weren't nothing unusual for a midsummer day and it being to the stern of the boat made the trip across the bay from Down Below to Trent fairly fast. It was a good day to be getting married.

The preacher didn't know we was coming but that didn't make no difference cause we know'd he'd be there. The island was a whole lot different then. Folks weren't able to get around quite so much and you could usually find somebody without no trouble at all, less they was out fishing or something.

Mag's mother and Mommie stood outside the Down Below church talking as we started to the shoreside to old man John Tolson's landing where his skiff was tied up. There weren't no real preacher in the Down Below church, just local folks filling in until we got another one. Poppie weren't feeling so good that day, so he had stayed home from the meeting. Old man Cale, Mag's father, went with us from the church to the skiff. Old man Cale helped Mag in the boat, then he turned to me and shook my hand. He never said nothing but with that smile on his face, I know'd he was proud for me to be marring Mag. She was the oldest of his five girls, so I was the first boy in his family. He always treated me good.

Old man John Tolson got in the skiff with us, untied her, and shoved her out in deep enough water, so she weren't dragging no more before we hoisted the sail. Once we got going it only took about an hour to get to Trent.

I don't remember much what me and Mag talked about going over. In July, it will be seventy years since we took that trip. I do remember Mag had on a right purdy dress made from some goods her father had brought back from Elizabeth City for her twenty-first birthday. I also remember feeling right strange out in the boat with a tie on, but I had to look good till we was married.

When we got to Trent, we docked the boat at the landing. Mag got out and tied her up while I helped to finish lower the sail. The preacher's house was right across the marsh. Old man John Tolson led the way. The mud fiddlers which was running all over the path took off in the marsh as we went by. It took all of two hours for the preacher to marry us and for his wife to feed us dinner before we headed back to Hatt'ras. The wind had breezed up right smart by that time, and the trip back took quite a bit longer than the one a going. Waves was washing over the bow of the skiff and by the time we reached old man John Tolson's landing, the only dry things on the boat was Mag's shoes and my tie which we had wrapped up in some oil cloth and had stuffed up in the bow.

By the time we fetched up to old man Cale's house, the sun had set, and there was just enough light for me and Mag to see to feed his two hogs. After supper, while we talked about the trip to Trent with old man Cale and Miss Mary, Mag's mother and her sisters, Kate and Sade, cleaned up the supper table. Her other two sisters was already dead—died when they was children.

Since I had to go fishing the next day, me and Mag went on over to Mommie and Poppie's and turned in. I had took care of Poppie and Mommie for the past seven years—since I was twelve years old. Me and Mag lived in the upstairs attic room of their house. The only thing 'tween us and the stars was the cedar shingles. We kept on taking care of them until they died. Then we moved over to old man Cale's after Miss Mary, Mag's mother, died and lived with him until he died. Miss Mary died of the same thing that Mag's got now—Kate died with it too.

It was while we was living Down Below at old man Cale's that our girls was born—Essie and Naomi. My goodness, I love those girls—one so dependent, the other so independent. Wonder why it is that two young'uns in the same family can be so different?

Boys, I would like to go out fishing just one more time, but I don't guess I ever will again. My leg hurts me to stand on it for too long of a time and besides Mag's too sick for me to leave her. She is too sick to even know that before long it will be our anniversary. Sure is funny what a difference seventy years makes. I can only get out of the house to cut grass when Essie's home from the store. She says Naomi will be here from Washington sometime this afternoon, and it will be so good to see her. She's going to stay down a while. Those girls of ours has been good to us.

Since Naomi's a nurse, maybe she can help Mag get better. I don't know, though; she ain't going to get no better. She ain't going to be here much longer. Mommie used to say that when a person got sick with whatever it was, that

took them to heaven, they was growing their angel wings. Mag's been growing
hers for ten years now.

Grandmom spread her angel wings two weeks later, gently departing from this world to whatever lies beyond. Just three years after that, Pop Pop would follow, his own wings ready to carry him on the same sacred journey.

On a crisp, cool morning in fall, Sister crossed the road. Shortly after Pop's passing, her steps were slow yet steady as she made her way toward her cousin Mary's house. Dressed as if for Sunday school and church, her Sunday best was crisp and neat, even though it was only Tuesday. That was the first sign—subtle, almost imperceptible—that she had begun growing her angel wings. The journey she was about to embark on would span more than thirteen long years, each marked by quiet moments of confusion, forgotten names, and lost memories. Like wings that unfold over time, it was a gradual transformation. This slow, steady decline carried her further from the person she once was, yet closer to the peace that awaited her.

A few years later, clad only in her pajamas, Mary spent the day lost in the confusion of the Alzheimer's unit of a nursing home, her eyes fixed on the courtyard outside the window. I imagine that the world around her felt distant, yet her thoughts swirled in disarray, intertwined with worry. She gazed at the familiar view, searching for anything that would make sense of the haze in her mind. Any visitor could see that her concern grew with each passing moment, a constant unease that her parents might not know where she was. A part of her memory had quietly slipped away, leaving only fragments of forgotten connections.

One hundred and twenty miles from Mary's institutional residence, a young attendant sits in front of the activity room of another nursing facility. She reaches for a ball falling from a rotating wire container into a linear trap below. She glances at it and shouts, "I, 16." She pauses and announces again, "I, 6." She picks up another ball and announces, "O, 67 . . . O, 6, 7." After another pause, she says, "B, 6 . . . B, 6." My mother hears the calls, but as much as she loves Bingo, they are meaningless.

She and Mary began their final journey around the same time in 1994.

On the quiet morning of May 8, 1999, just as the first light of Saturday began to soften the world's edges, my phone rang. My brother delivered the message I knew was inevitable: our precious mother's angel wings had fully formed, ready to carry her beyond the reach of earthly pain. With a peace that had eluded her during months of suffering, she left us, reunited with Pop

Mama

Pop, Grandmom, and Sister, joining those who had gone before her in what-ever gentle place exists beyond our understanding. My brother and I grieve her loss deeply, yet there's solace in knowing she is free at last from the relent-less grip of the disease that had slowly taken so much from her away from us. We hold on to the hope that she is surrounded by the love of her family who passed before her, embraced by those who cherish her just as we do, and is now at rest, her spirit whole once more.

Mary followed soon after, her spirit soaring as she reunited with Mama and the souls of her loved ones, embraced by the peace that had awaited her.

CHAPTER 16

Going to a Fire

Sometimes, in the quiet before dawn, you might hear them creaking, stretching, and groaning as they rouse to the sunrise. In the twilight calm after a stormy day, they settle and sigh. In the magic between midnight and morning, they are gently vigilant and perhaps whisper to each other, "remember when . . .?"

They are the old houses of Hatteras, and, together, they are the heart of the village.

These houses are symbols of a unique and spirited lifestyle, one often arduous yet romantic—a way of life that sustained our parents, grandparents, and their parents and is now rapidly succumbing to change and challenge. These houses and their companions—the old boats and the family cemeteries—have stories to tell us. The roles they played in the history of Hatteras Village deserve recognition. Their preservation honors our heritage and carries the spirit of the past into the future. — "Heritage of Hatteras Village" by Linda Elizabeth Nunn. Commissioned by the Hatteras Village Civic Association.

7 a.m., March 10, 2012

With all the joys of life, there also come moments of sadness. This morning, just after daybreak, I felt a wave of sorrow as I took my camera and stepped out the door to visit an old friend. I knew it would be our last time together.

I can't remember the first time I met her; time has erased that memory.

The Henry Christina Stowe house

However, I recall my Grandmom taking my hand on a hot summer day in the 1940s and embarking on an endless mile-long walk along the soft sandy road from our house to visit her at Sticky Bottom. We lived "up the road" at the northern end of Hatteras Village, while my friend spent her life in Sticky Bottom, the village's southern end.

As I wandered down her lane this morning, the only sound was the relentless, cold north wind blowing through the trees. Framed by gnarled oaks, yaupons, and water bushes, she gradually came into view, sitting in the same spot she had occupied for over 150 years. She is a proud lady, and rightly so. Today, she is the oldest house in Hatteras Village, but tomorrow, she will pass that title on to another.

Around 1860, Henry and Christina Stowe built the home. At the turn of the century, the house underwent substantial remodeling. Along with a detached kitchen, a second story was built. A new kitchen, dining area, and bedroom were erected after the detached kitchen was demolished in the

1930s. Like many Hatteras houses, holes were bored in the floor, allowing tidewater to enter and exit the structure quickly during storms, preventing it from floating off its foundation.

One of Henry Stowe's daughters, Janette, spent her ninety-nine years living in this old house. She and her husband, Irv, raised their family here. In his younger years, Mr. Irv served as the captain of the *Ethel*. This freight boat operated between Hatteras and Elizabeth City. He was also a boatbuilder and later fished for a living. Miss Janette kept busy raising seven children and worked as the island midwife, delivering three generations of children on Hatteras and Ocracoke islands, many of whom share her name. As customary, the Hatteras United Methodist Church bell tolled upon her death to honor her ninety-nine years as a community member.

This morning, the Henry and Christina Stowe house lacked the determination that had allowed it to withstand the elements it had faced over the past century and a half.

Neglect and time had taken their toll on the old house—her foundation sagged, her timbers bowed, and her paint cracked and peeled. For the past decade, she had been left unattended. Occasionally, a curious passerby would peer through her windows, walk around her footprint, and wonder what stories she had to tell. However, the tide, time, and termite damage was not reversible. She was dying, and nothing could bring her back.

I snapped a few photos and ran my fingers along her weathered walls, reminiscing about my visits with Miss Janette. With a heavy heart, I slowly turned away from my weary old friend, knowing she would be another cherished memory of Hatteras by tomorrow.

10 a.m., March 11, 2012

The house, this landmark of the village is ablaze—and not just any historical landmark, but the oldest one.

The Hatteras Volunteer Fire Department arrived early, prepared to confront the unpredictable challenge of a wind-driven blaze. For the new recruits, it was merely another training session.

The flames quickly engulfed her, and with a gentle crash, she succumbed to the inferno. The north wind carried her ashes across the marsh and out to the sound.

Remnants of the Stowe house after the fire

Miss Janette's great-grandson and his wife, the former owners of the old house, stood by with tears as their family treasure turned to smoke and smoldering embers. They inherited a heavy burden, but their brave attempts to restore the old house soon faced the reality that nothing lasts forever.

This house's role in the history of Hatteras Village deserves no more credit than any other old house. All deserve to be honored because they provided comfort to those who lived within their walls and a place of beauty for those who passed by.

We will miss you, my dear friend.

CHAPTER 17

Going Home

The exact construction date of my grandparents' family home remains a mystery. However, we believe builders constructed it in the early twentieth century. Due to poor title records from that era, it was likely around 1902.

After my grandparents married in 1903, they moved into the second floor of my great-grandfather's house, where they cared for my grandmother's father until his passing in 1923. The house stood on a slight rise known as "Chally's Hill" in an area locals called "Sticky Bottom" at the southern end of Hatteras Village. The second floor was unfinished at that time, containing only a modest bedroom.

After the passing of my grandmother's father, my grandparents recognized the need for a better home to raise their children. In April of that year, they purchased a property at the northern end of the village, just across the sandy road from my grandmother's sister's home. They acquired a 4.5-acre plot of land with a house elevated about a foot off the ground on wooden piers for $400. This modest house featured four rooms—two on the ground floor and two upstairs. The front included a spacious porch. Upon entering through the front door, a hallway ran the entire length of the house, separating the two downstairs rooms. One was a guest bedroom, while my grandparents referred to the other as the "sitting room."

A staircase in the hallway led to two upstairs bedrooms, separated by a small hall-like area my grandparents affectionately called the "scuttle." They slept in the southern bedroom while their daughters shared the northern

My grandparents' first house, circa 1923

one. Behind the main house stood a separate kitchen, a standard precaution to prevent fires from spreading, and the privy.

When my grandparents' girls reached adolescence, they started an extension project for their house. At the front of the home, they created a cozy living room surrounded on three sides by a porch, our pizer. There were multiple side tables, a sofa, and an armchair purchased for this new space. They bought a freestanding Victrola, complete with a variety of records fea-

My grandparents' house, circa 1972

turing the hottest music of the time, to complete the room. Their goal was to provide a comfortable setting for their children to entertain friends in while still being able to monitor their interactions and activities closely.

My grandparents and their daughters had to seek shelter in the upstairs bedrooms after the house was inundated by increasing storm seas following the 1937 hurricane. To protect it from potential hurricane flooding, they then raised the house a couple of feet. Instead of standing one foot above the ground, it then stood three.

Sometime after my birth in 1941, my grandparents expanded their house by adding two rooms at the back: a kitchen and an extra bedroom. With these additions, the house had two bedrooms downstairs—one for my parents and one for me. However, after my younger brother was born in 1946, he eventually moved into my room to stay close to our parents.

My grandfather recalled that the old detached kitchen was torn down and thrown into the ditch behind the toilet. The family gave this waterway its unflattering name because they positioned the outdoor toilet over it. My brother and I finally added a bathroom after we took ownership of the house.

As a teenager, I once peeked through a crack in the scuttle wall and discovered an unfinished attic room above the living room. Excited by the possibility of having my own space, I asked my grandfather if he would finish the room so I could use it as my bedroom. He agreed, and it became my sanctuary—the first room I could call my own after years of sharing a bedroom with my brother at our parents' house until I left for college.

Hatteras Village was the sturdy trunk from which the branches of my cherished memories grew. There, rooted in their love and the slow pace of life on that isolated island, I spent those idyllic summers with my grandparents. As my remembrances have recorded here, it was a hidden gem back then, cradled by the sea and untouched by progress. With no paved roads, electricity, telephones, television, or indoor plumbing—and no tourists in sight—it remained a quiet sanctuary where whispering tides and golden sands stretched undisturbed. As my younger brother grew, he eventually joined me for these summers—two leaves sprouting from the same branch, carried by the salty breeze of adventure.

After our grandparents passed away in the 1970s and Aunt Essie in 1998, the family estate became ours. For the next few decades, it remained our cherished summer retreat. In the 1980s, my brother and I purchased a vacant lot next door, with the intention of building an additional home for one of us.

After thirty-seven years of investing in public education, I decided to retire. In 1999, I sold my home of thirty-three years in New Bern and committed to making Hatteras my permanent residence. Curious about my brother's plans, I asked whether he had ever considered living in Hatteras full-time. His initial response was, "Probably not." I then proposed a trade: He could keep the beloved ancestral home as his summer retreat while I would take full ownership of our neighboring property to build my new permanent home.

At fifty-nine, after a lifetime as a bachelor, I unexpectedly met the missing piece that completed the puzzle of my life. While I was in the early stages of building my home, I visited the local electrical co-op to set up a temporary power service. I had no idea my future wife was sitting behind the reception desk when I stepped inside. The moment I saw her, I was captivated. When I admitted that I knew nothing about installing electricity at the building site, she confidently and professionally guided me through the steps. She was radiant, with a kindness that felt like sunlight breaking through newly settled clouds. Her laughter was warm, her presence effortless, and something within me shifted from the moment I saw her. The rest is history. Love found me when I least expected it. I was no longer the confirmed bachelor I had always been. Instead, I was a man completely, undeniably smitten, walking a path I had never imagined—one that led straight to her. And when she became my wife, I realized that life, even at 59, could still surprise me in the most extraordinary ways.

After the builders completed the new home, my brother realized how much he loved the charm of life in Hatteras. Upon retiring, he and his wife undertook an ambitious renovation of the old house—raising it ten feet, insulating the walls, adding extra rooms, a second bathroom, and spacious decks.

In a location that has always embodied our best memories, my brother, our spouses, and I now enjoy these golden years together. Each day is wrapped in the warmth of the past as if the air we breathe carries echoes of the moments we cherish. On quiet mornings and leisurely afternoons, I still hear the voices of my childhood neighbors, their laughing and remarks echoing like gentle whispers from another time. Their lives, now woven into history, evoke a bittersweet nostalgia—sometimes bringing a tear to my eye and, at other times, filling my heart with smiles as soft and precious as the days we shared.

"Sister" by Clifford Swain

Here is a remembrance of Sister, our Aunt Essie, written by my brother, Clifford Swain. My brother and I called her "Sister." Although she wasn't our sister, she was our aunt. Her given name was Essie Mae Wade. Most folks in Hatteras knew her simply as "Miss Essie."

She was the eldest daughter of Clifford and Maggie Wade, a family with deep roots on Hatteras Island. Her only sister was my mother, Naomi Wade Swain. The two daughters affectionately called each other "Sister," as many older folks used to do. By default, my brother and I picked it up too. I can't remember ever calling her anything but "Sister." This did lead to some confusion in later years with healthcare professionals who struggled to understand our relationship. Many adopted "Sister" as her name as well. She meant so much more to us than just an aunt.

She never married. She devoted her entire life to her family, church, and job. We thought of her as a second mother. I selfishly prayed that she would stay unmarried, as I didn't want to share her with anyone else. Little did I know that she was already a surrogate parent to many children in the village.

Her only job during her eighty-six years was as an employee of what used to be known as "Burrus Red and White" in Hatteras Village. She began with her first employer, Mr. Dolph Burrus. The small general store was simply called "Mr. Dolph's." Over the years, "Mr. Dolph's" became "Bill's" when his son Bill Burrus took over. Later, the grandsons, Dale and Allen Burrus, ran "Burrus Red and White." Today, it is known as the Village Red and White

Market and is under new ownership. The Burrus family was more than just an employer; they became an integral part of each other's lives. Sister cared deeply for the Burrus family, and they, in turn, cared for her. She was a fixture at the store for most of her adult life. At her funeral several years ago, Allen Burrus reflected on Ms. Essie's impact on his family and the community. He shared how every child who bought anything from Ms. Essie received a lesson in math, whether they wanted it or not, delivered in slow motion. Barefoot children eager to enjoy their small candy or drink purchases were required to repeat, number for number, the addition and subtraction resulting from their purchases.

She dedicated herself to teaching Sunday school and Bible school, nurturing and loving every child under her care.

Her life was a ministry, and everyone who crossed her slow yet gracious path fondly remembered her. She loved Hatteras Village and all the people who lived there. Sister was one of those rare individuals who refused to harbor a bad thought about anyone. In a time when negativity is so commonplace, Sister stands out as saintly to me. We could not get her to utter a "bad word" or condemn anyone, no matter how serious the offense.

She focused solely on the positive potential and left the negativity for others to debate. She lived her life simply, with dignity and a natural inner beauty.

Many years ago, we packed her belongings to bring her to live closer to us because of her declining health. During this process, my brother discovered a handwritten poem she had written. At some point in her young adult life, she composed this poem to express her feelings for her hometown. She never had it printed, and to my knowledge, she never shared it with anyone. She created this poem while living without fanfare or attention. It is a treasure to us.

This poem holds even more meaning as Hatteras Village recovers from the horrific storm damage caused by hurricanes. Through this poem, Miss Essie, Sister, continues to give to the place she holds so dear, from the past, from a native, from a soul that never dies. The best guess is that it was written in the early 1930s.

Sister and Mama

At Hatteras

Poem by Essie Wade

There's plenty of Sea and Air and Sky,
At Hatteras
But there's little of Earth to gladden the eye,
At Hatteras
Where the Moonlight gilds the silent night
And ever the booming Surf gleams white
As it tears and claws at the Diamond Shoals,
The restless grave of a thousand souls,
Off Hatteras
Where the ceaseless song of the nasty deep
Lures to repose, and I sleep and sleep
As with a poppy heart the whole nightlong
Till the Mockingbird sings his morning song
At Hatteras
There's a plenty of sun in the vaulted blue
At Hatteras
There's a boundless freedom in all we do
At Hatteras
Where simple human nature rules
Where art and convention know no school
Where nothing is ever done today
That can tomorrow be put away
At Hatteras
Here where the sea gull screams and scolds
Where a thousand wild geese
Honk their wail
In the teeth of a screaming screeching gale
At Hatteras
Barren remote and bleak and lone
Still to these folks it is Home, Sweet Home
At Hatteras

Acknowledgments

Clyde Edgerton, Leigh Ballance, and I forged a lifelong friendship in our early twenties while serving as counselors at a camp for children with mental challenges—an experience that shaped us in ways we could never have imagined. Clyde became a celebrated novelist and professor, captivating readers with his rich Southern storytelling. However, his creativity extends beyond that—he is a gifted musician and a talented artist. Yet, it was his writing that ignited a creative desire in both Leigh and me, encouraging us to explore the realm of storytelling.

Leigh, who recently passed away, left behind an incredible legacy—not only as a successful banker and entrepreneur but also as the author of the charming children's book, *The Secrets of Gum Swamp*. As for me, after thirty-seven years navigating the "blackboard jungle," I like to think that I, too, have made a lasting impact on the hundreds of students who sat in my classes, learning about the incredible beauty of science.

At the heart of it all, Clyde's inspiration nudged two wannabe writers out of their comfort zones, urging us to create something real and lasting.

Throughout my writing journey, I have been fortunate to have an incredible support team. Many have read my stories and offered encouragement, but none more so than my brother, Clifford, and my wife, Anne. Clifford provided me with a wealth of material to write about and has been my faithful cheerleader. My wife, Anne, has also been a cheerleader and a tireless editor with unwavering patience—reading and rereading my work, catching typos, grammatical errors, and misplaced commas.

A special debt of gratitude goes to Gee Gee Rosell, the passionate owner of Buxton Village Books on Hatteras Island. Publishing my work was never part of the plan—I was content simply to put my thoughts on paper. But when I shared my manuscript with Gee Gee, she saw something more. She became the driving force behind my decision to take the leap and share my words with the world.

Sandra Hughes Benton is a remarkable talent and friend. With more than twenty-five years of experience in marketing, advertising, and photography, she designed the cover of the first edition of the book. She runs S. Hughes Imaging LLC. Her photography is captivating, and her art is masterful.

An outstanding debt of gratitude goes to Jan Dawson, a popular novelist whose books' themes are centered on Hatteras Island. She was a treasure trove of information and encouragement, who helped me avoid many pitfalls on this journey. Many thanks also go to Cindy Evans, a very dear friend, for reading the final manuscript and contributing valuable suggestions and pointing out overlooked errors. And finally, a special thanks to Lynn York whose professional editing skills were so valuable, the polish to the final draft of this project.